Making Virtual Reality a Reality

Making Virtual Reality a Reality

Designing Educational Initiatives in Libraries with Emerging Technologies

Alison Valk, Ximin Mi, and Ashley L. Schick

BLOOMSBURY LIBRARIES UNLIMITED
NEW YORK • LONDON • OXFORD • NEW DELHI • SYDNEY

BLOOMSBURY LIBRARIES UNLIMITED
Bloomsbury Publishing Inc
1385 Broadway, New York, NY 10018, USA
50 Bedford Square, London, WC1B 3DP, UK
29 Earlsfort Terrace, Dublin 2, Ireland

BLOOMSBURY, BLOOMSBURY LIBRARIES UNLIMITED and the Diana logo are trademarks of Bloomsbury Publishing Plc

First published in the United States of America 2023

Library of Congress Cataloging in Publication Control Number: 2022055309

ISBN: PB: 978-1-4408-7897-8
ePDF: 978-1-4408-7898-5
eBook: 979-8-216-17195-9

Typeset by Westchester Publishing Services, LLC
Printed and bound in the United States of America

To find out more about our authors and books visit www.bloomsbury.com and sign up for our newsletters.

For all the students and the inspiring educators I have collaborated with over the years, and finally for my dad, who always encouraged me in my writing, I learned so much from you. —Alison

This book is dedicated to the very bright and curious Georgia Tech students. You inspire and drive me to do better at my job, and thus, this book. Also to my 19-month-old daughter, Bella. Without you I'd pull my hair so hard while writing it, but you got that taken care of. —Ximin

To Andrew, Sophia, and Ember, with love. —Ashley

Contents

ONE

Making Virtual Reality a Reality

INTRODUCTION

But what is reality? The concepts behind virtual reality date back to the 1800s with the invention of stereoscopes. Stanley G. Weinbaum's short story "*Pygmalion's Spectacles*," published in 1935, described a pair of goggles that transported the protagonist to another reality. The glasses allowed people to experience tactile sensations, sights, and smells outside their own current experiences. Despite being published in 1935, the story depicted futuristic experiences—not unlike present-day emerging technologies—such as virtual and augmented reality. As with many technological advances, a fictional story gave innovators the seeds of future ideas. The concepts in the story gave birth to some of the modern technologies we are familiar with today (Figure 1-1).

Transitioning from science fiction to science, the term "virtual" was first used in 1959 in reference to computers, as in "not physically existing but made to appear by software" (Online Etymology Dictionary, n.d.). Some of the early versions of virtual reality devices can be found at the retroTECH lab in the Georgia Tech library. The retroTECH lab maintains a variety of technological apparatuses from "slide rules to Sega Genesis, as well as emulations of retro platforms" that visitors can interact with as seen in Figure 1-2 (Georgia Tech Library n.d.). Some of the immersive gadgets that prefigure today's virtual reality head-mounted displays are a part of the collection. Stereoscopes were created by Charles Wheatstone in 1838 and later refined by David Brewster. The stereoscope works by aligning an image "from two slightly different perspectives" in front of

Figure 1-1 Stereoscope and View-Master in the retroTECH collection

each eye (Thompson 2017). Just like how regular bifocal perception works, the brain is able to combine the two offset images into a single three-dimensional (3D) scene (Thompson 2017). In the 1800s, these images could be hand-drawn or photographic, capturing exotic jungles, famous landmarks, astronomical objects, or celebrity portraits. The stereoscope was even promoted for its "uniquely instructive" educational use in the late nineteenth-century classroom (Thompson 2017).

> *"The first effect of looking at a good photograph through the stereoscope is a surprise such as no painting ever produced," gushed Oliver Wendell Holmes, the American surgeon and author, in an 1859 Atlantic essay. "The mind feels its way into the very depths of the picture. The scraggy branches of a tree in the foreground run out at us as if they would scratch our eyes out."* (Thompson 2017)

In the 1930s, Sawyer's, and later Mattel, introduced the View-Master, a plastic, mechanized form of the stereoscope that remained popular through the end of the twentieth century. Different manufacturers produced numerous varieties of plastic casings that held a "reel" disc of paired photos that could be mechanically advanced in front of the eyepieces (Clatworthy, n.d.).

Figure 1-2 Analog gadgets from the retroTECH collection

A brief fad of 3D movies had a golden age in the 1950s, where audience members would wear anaglyph glasses that divide the images for each eye by color (usually red and cyan) as in Figure 1-3. The other major form of 3D film uses polarization to control the orientation of light waves reaching each eye (Patterson 2009). In an even more immersive experience, the Sensorama Simulator, introduced in 1962, ran a 3D film in a special single-user projector apparatus that also emitted vibrations, audio tracks, airflow, and scents around the viewer for a multisensory experience (Turi 2014). Theater-sized "4D" rides offer similar experiences to theme park visitors in the twenty-first century.

Devices created specifically for virtual reality (VR) and augmented reality (AR) have been around since the 1960s, mainly known in the areas of gaming and entertainment. However, most recently, they are being incorporated into industry and education. But what do we mean by these different types of realities? Virtual reality is characterized by immersive environments. The user is completely immersed in a computer-generated simulated environment, often using a special headset. Augmented reality incorporates the user's physical environment and superimposes elements such as sounds, visuals, and objects into the real-world surroundings.

Figure 1-3 Anaglyph Glasses

In addition to headsets, smartphones and mobile devices can be used with AR. There is also mixed reality (MR). Like augmented reality, mixed reality allows for digital images to be layered onto the user's current environment, but MR also allows the user to manipulate those images. Some forms of this technology are classified as XR, or extended reality, a catch-all term that encompasses any type of physical-plus-virtual immersive experience.

How can virtual technologies make learning more engaging and productive? And what role are these emerging technologies playing in education? Kavanagh et al. (2017) show that VR applications have a positive effect on students' motivation and enjoyment, help them focus on tasks longer, and help them gain deeper learning experiences. Emerging technologies are poised to become a critical part of secondary and higher education. They have been used across disciplines, including health-related, general education, science, engineering, and others. Trends of note include gamification, AR/VR, robotics, and AI (artificial intelligence), just to name a few. Gamification is a concept commonly associated with school-age children, but gamified learning can also be used effectively in higher education. Students can earn points or badges by reaching milestones within a team environment. Having a scaffolded learning system in place alongside gamified problem-solving can keep students engaged regardless of their education level. One of the Georgia Tech Library's case studies that will be discussed in greater detail later in this book had students not only playing a game but creating a game with an integrated reward system to help them play and learn through the VR experience.

Virtual and augmented reality are transforming the STEM (science, technology, engineering, and mathematics) curriculum. For example, at the higher education level, Stanford University's *Ocean Acidification Experience* allows students to understand and experience the effect of carbon dioxide on marine life. The project's mission is to use VR in research and to "improve everyday life, such as conservation, empathy, and communications systems" (Craig and Georgieva 2017).

Middle schools and high schools are also beginning to develop preparatory programs to familiarize their students with technologies they will be introduced to in college. As a result, students are being exposed to emerging technologies earlier and earlier. For example, the Mount Vernon school in Atlanta, Georgia, has been the *Dell/Alienware flagship virtual reality studio* since 2018, collaborating with corporations and nonprofits to give students real-world experiences with XR. "The lab, conceived of and now managed by students, is being used to influence learning through empathy. Market-ready prototypes and public exhibits have already been developed for health-care companies like CHOA [Children's Healthcare of Atlanta] and social justice organizations like The Center for Civil and Human Rights" (Mount Vernon School, n.d.).

Emerging technologies encourage critical thinking and open-ended investigation, and provide students with immersive experiences that allow them to apply concepts they may have otherwise only learned about in theory. Platforms are being developed that allow students to problem solve within a simulated science lab (Labster, n.d.). Students can familiarize themselves with basic lab safety procedures while learning from their mistakes in an environment without real consequences. Educators are also using immersive technologies to explain complex topics to a broad audience. For example, physicists are using VR to explain concepts such as string theory. Scientists and engineers from NASA use VR to visualize other areas of the solar system (Craig and Georgieva 2017). Ultimately, immersive and emerging technologies are catalysts for interdisciplinary collaborations and encourage restructuring of the traditional classroom learning models.

Emerging technologies are reinventing how students synthesize information. When we think about a restructuring of the traditional learning models, this includes who is involved in the student's learning process. One of the many challenges on college campuses today is finding new ways to engage students with their course material, as well as expanding a student's worldview beyond disciplinary silos. Further involving librarians, artists, industry professionals, and community leaders in classrooms and in curriculum development enriches interdisciplinary study and will provide students with a more holistic educational experience (Valk 2019). Librarians are trained to see how concepts are categorized and connected and recognize the web of associations. Libraries by nature touch on every discipline, and often librarians can recognize relevant synergies and beneficial partnerships ahead of the curve. Librarians also have new roles outside of the public perception of simply managing collections and providing research assistance. New focuses of librarianship have expanded into the space of multimedia skills, educational technology, data science, and many more new areas. These roles are reflective of the changing educational landscape and the resources required to accomplish professional and academic goals. These qualities make libraries an ideal location to foster student curiosity in emerging technologies such as AR/VR. Artists, in addition to librarians, are finding their place in the classroom as well. Teaching artists are individuals who are both practicing artists and educators (Saraniero 2008, 21). Rather than artists who train students to become artists, teaching artists frequently "provide learning opportunities in and through the arts rather than providing skill-building instruction in the arts" (Saraniero 2008, 22). Artists are partnering with classroom teachers in a variety of disciplines to bring creative content into the academic classroom to enhance learning outcomes for students.

We will elaborate further on the roles of artists, librarians, and various educators who play key roles in the development of new pedagogies and programming as this book progresses. The book is structured as part reflection on lessons learned and part handbook for integrating emerging technologies such as VR and AR into your organization's programming. Tailored for those just getting started, the book begins with a retrospective on our own projects and key takeaways from those experiences. While covering the perspective of both higher education and secondary school, we will discuss assessment and resource evaluation, technology requirements, and ultimately how we as educators can foster student-centric research and learning.

INNOVATIVE PROGRAMMING IN LIBRARIES

Libraries are no longer just a central location for traditional resources such as books and journals. Whether an academic library, a school library, or a public library, they are becoming a hub for the exchange of collective knowledge. Programming and services build on the idea of active learning, reflection, discussion, and community engagement. Librarians and educators are working hand in hand with students, community members, and patrons to explore new ideas, technologies, and research approaches.

For instance, public libraries are expanding their programming to include innovative services such as seed libraries. A seed library is a place where patrons can get plant seeds for free or at a low cost, and in return community members collect some of the seeds from their resulting plants at the end of the growing season. Often, educational programming on gardening is included in the process. Peekhaus (2018) describes the role of seed libraries in public libraries as "community access points that are moving beyond their traditional information gatekeeping roles to deliver innovative services and resources that hold out the potential to contribute to more resilient, healthier and better-fed communities." Additionally, seed libraries are representative of programming where community engagement is not seen as transactional; members and librarians share collective knowledge on community gardens, and the patrons ultimately give back to the library by contributing to the future of the seed library.

School libraries are incorporating makerspaces and lending programs, including tool libraries, into their curriculum. Based on concepts associated with constructivist learning theory, makerspaces encourage learning as an active process where community members acquire knowledge through hands-on experiences. Makerspaces are often a site for peer-learning activities where students learn from more experienced users or peer mentors. Users of the space are encouraged to try working with equipment and hardware that support anything from carpentry to engineering or electronics. These interdisciplinary spaces give anyone the opportunity to experiment with tools they may not have access to, typically. Makerspaces often incorporate events and programming that support the use of these specialized tools. Like unique programs such as the seed libraries, these makerspaces become centers for communities of practice.

Not unlike school libraries, academic libraries provide access to computer peripheries and equipment that support the use of certain types of computer software in course assignments and campus research. This could be anything from drawing tablets with styluses that are used with illustration software to graphing calculators or high-powered cameras. In some cases, academic libraries are making hardware such as virtual reality headsets available to the campus community. Making this hardware available allows students to use certain software more effectively to create projects they wouldn't be able to otherwise create. Users check out these devices as they would the library's traditional print resources. The main objective is providing equal access to these resources regardless of a person's discipline or background. Additionally, the libraries are cultivating curiosity by exposing users to experiences and equipment they might not otherwise have an opportunity to experiment with.

One quality all these types of libraries have in common is that rather than leaving students on their own to discover information on when and how to use the equipment, librarians are stepping in and proactively engaging with their community to develop programming that encourages research and educational exploration. As libraries step out of the passive role of gatekeeper and into one of partnership with the community they serve, this sets the stage for meaningful collaboration.

While it can be argued that libraries are expanding rapidly and trying to meet too many needs, ultimately, regardless of modality or format, the overarching goal of libraries is to provide users access to resources to support their educational experiences. As such, environmental scans of research methods and modes are critical to the development of new services and programming. As the mission of the American Library Association states, our goals are "to provide leadership for the development, promotion, and improvement of library and information services and the profession of librarianship in order to enhance learning and ensure access to information for all" (ALA 2008).

GEORGIA TECH CASE STUDY

As mentioned previously, library offerings have grown, in many cases providing access to emerging technologies including resources supporting augmented reality and virtual reality. While providing access to these technologies, libraries also offer information and instruction on suitable use cases.

Given the innovative research happening on the college campuses, the role that libraries play in introducing modern technologies to the academic community is even more important. Academic libraries support the entire campus and are open to all regardless of discipline or department. This access to needed tools and resources is key. Users of the library never have to feel they must be part of advanced research or must be highly skilled in order to experiment with professional technologies. A library can provide users with their first low-stakes experience utilizing technologies and software that at first seem daunting. However, through self-paced exploration, students can become skilled and, ultimately, empowered. Georgia Tech developed such an educational environment through their own instructional programming.

While reflecting on our experiences of integrating emerging technologies into the educational programming at Georgia Tech, we were able to develop a blueprint for instruction, service design, and library-centric research that positively impacts the student learning experience. This blueprint can be adapted and utilized in a variety of educational settings on a large or small scale. Our chapters are structured to guide readers through the main elements of this pedagogical blueprint as well as course design prompts or considerations.

In Georgia Tech Library's for-credit research classes, the librarians partner with other academic departments and programs on campus to facilitate and lead student-centered research. These initiatives are building on the pedagogical benefits and concepts that make up the framework of embedded librarianship. Kubelka explains "the rise of embedded librarianship on academic campuses illustrates the departure from one-shot library instruction classes, which have historically limited the librarian's ability to impact student outcomes in a meaningful way. Strong partnerships between faculty and librarians are at the heart of the embedded librarianship approach, allowing librarians to transcend the 'consultant' role with sustained involvement that integrates librarians into the planning and preparation of course work. These collaborative efforts not only build stronger connections between faculty and librarians, but they also improve the student learning experience and increase student engagement" (2016).

Georgia Tech librarians and archivists are taking the concept of embedded librarianship one step further, leading and facilitating research on interdisciplinary studies. Libraries are, at their core, interdisciplinary spaces (Valk 2019). Integral to an academic library's role on campus is the ability to serve and support their community members regardless of their chosen discipline or background, while providing equal access to resources. The Georgia Tech Library's for-credit research sections give students an opportunity to grow their research and experiences beyond what is expected in their majors or expected degree tracks. This approach strives to expand horizons and diversify the student learning experience.

Some of the Georgia Tech Library's early involvement in for-credit classes began with a collaboration between the Georgia Tech librarians and Georgia Tech's computational media program. Computational media majors focus on work that supports them in the design and development of video games, animation, special effects, and user interfaces. Computational media alumni have gone on to work for major video game studios and interactive-media firms. The Bachelor of Science in computational media (BSCM) is a joint offering between the College of Computing and the School of Literature, Media, and Communication (Georgia Tech Computational Media 2022).

This work with the computational media program aligned with Library Next, a major Georgia Tech initiative. Library Next is a continuing analysis, based on purposeful interactions with faculty and students, of service gaps that the library can fill to address changing campus teaching and research needs. Through Library Next, Georgia Tech is creating a new version of a technology-focused, need-based, and data-driven research library for the twenty-first century. Begun several years ago as a library building renovation, Library Next is now a major transformation of the library's vision and a redesign of services. All components of a research library, the inspirational physical and digital environments, curated scholarly content, outstanding services, and information expertise continue to change as the research and teaching goals and aspirations of Georgia Tech change (Murray-Rust et al. 2019).

In 2018, the Georgia Tech Library started integrating augmented reality and virtual reality into the organization's suite of services. At the time, the library had few devices, one Oculus Rift (the first consumer version of Rift) and one VIVE. A few 360 Utopias and Leap Motion controllers were added to this collection later. With no previous experience in supporting these technologies, the library began experimenting with open game play and building a framework for service development. To experiment with open game play, the service team downloaded educational games on a library STEAM account installed at the VR workstations and opened the workstations for students to experiment and experience immersive environments.

As more students gained hands-on experience with the equipment, they approached the library team with questions regarding virtual reality and augmented reality in their coursework. Technology-focused librarians identified the potential benefits of making these devices available to campus for teaching, learning, and research. These conversations led to the AR/VR research course for undergraduates. The design of this course concept was based on the earlier feedback collected from students: give them first-hand development experience by creating their own projects.

For the purpose of this course, the librarians were looking for students with an interest in combining technologies with creative artistic work. The team initially reached out to the computational media program to recruit students for this class. This program focuses on computing, the history of media, and developing skills in visual design, which makes it a perfect fit for a partnership with the library. Started in spring 2018, the library's emerging technologies research course opened to campus as a non-lecture, hands-on cohort of students who could work in groups or individually. The objective of this course is for students to carve out their own project ideas and implement them with VR and other advanced technologies throughout the semester.

To understand students' project interests and their technical background, the librarians offer an information session before the class starts each semester. This session gives the librarians an opportunity to explain to students the class design and workload. It also allows students to express what they want to learn and accomplish in the class. These sessions serve as a window for librarians and students to align their understanding and expectations. These early interactions provide librarians with a mechanism to evaluate students' skills and manage project scope.

Once the semester starts, the first few weeks center on discussing project ideas, group formation, and peer review of project designs. About one-fourth of the way (four weeks) into the semester, students submit a proposal of their projects as a group or individually. This proposal includes the project design, the device and software of their choice, their collaboration plan and storage options. The proposals serve as general guides for the librarians and students to follow through the semester. Students are allowed to make minor adjustments during implementation. At the end of the semester, students submit a working VR project along with a final report detailing the design, technologies used, major milestones, challenges, how the final project differs from the proposal, lessons learned, possible next steps of work, and access to the work if applicable. In some cases, project ideas were linked to teaching and learning or services on campus.

This emerging technology research section is regularly limited to three to five students per semester, which allows the librarians and instructors to provide focused conversations and individualized attention to students regarding their project. Over the past semesters, student designs have ranged from a virtual campus tour to a campaign for VR application in research, as well as a virtual escape room experience in Sweden and meditation in a virtual garden. Having learned from new project design ideas during previous semesters, the librarians updated the class to be semi-structured, holding discussion-driven meetings where students share useful resources, refine project designs, update implementation progress, and ask questions.

In addition to an improvement to the course structure, a device upgrade was also necessary. Georgia Tech Library's AR/VR devices remain a small collection due to limited funding. Over the course of the program, however, the librarians were able to upgrade some of the hardware to newer versions to reflect the ongoing changes of AR/VR devices. In 2019, the library added Oculus Rift S and Oculus Quest 1. As hardware technologies change, VR devices have been evolving to become both more lightweight and untethered. This is a positive change for developers as it makes the devices easier to access and use. To keep up with this trend and guarantee students have the newer devices, in 2021, the library acquired Oculus Quest 2, the newer version of Oculus untethered options. Over the years, the library retired the older, tethered devices (VIVE and Rifts) after they got damaged or lost some of their functionality. Matching the small device collection to the small class size affords the librarians enough time to have in-depth discussions with each project team. At the same time, students have more freedom to choose the device they wish to use.

Students from this class had overwhelmingly positive feedback. One exchange student from Sweden mentioned that, thanks to the hands-on approach, he learned so much from the class that he decided to go into the field. It was, in fact, in the library's class that he learned the most skills relevant to his career ambitions while studying at Georgia Tech as an exchange student.

BENEFITS AND USES OF VR IN K–12 CLASSROOMS

Higher education is not the only environment piloting these emerging technologies. K–12 is also rapidly integrating them into the curriculum, giving students early experiences with coding, 3D scanning, graphic design, and 360 cameras, just to name a few. Immersive technologies are helping K–12 students with soft skills including collaboration, teamwork, critical thinking, and problem-solving (Zimmerman 2022). Additional research is being done on how AR/VR technologies can be used to aid students with learning disabilities or different learning styles (CTD Institute 2018).

Librarians and educators in a K–12 environment have similar considerations to higher ed programs when developing VR programs at their schools, while they also must adapt this programming to the unique circumstances of a younger audience. K–12 students are often very perceptive and sophisticated, and in some cases only slight content modifications will be necessary. Educators of young children may need to consider how they discuss with students the process of distinguishing between real-life and virtual experiences (Slayden and Graham 2018, 25). Overall, the technical and material challenges of implementing emerging technology programs—for example, finding a budget, collaborating with other departments, managing larger classes, working within short class periods—will frequently need the most adaptations from higher ed to K–12.

Given those challenges, when is it best to integrate emerging technologies into a busy K–12 classroom? Emerging technologies can be most useful to students when the integration takes advantage of the immersive aspect of the technologies, including activities that engage the body or activities that benefit from insights given by a 3D model (as opposed to information on a flat 2D surface). In all cases, the integration should "bolster the curriculum we already have" in the classroom (Jacobson 2019). The integration should not seek to "wow" the students at every turn—students consume so much professionally created media that that is nearly an impossible goal—but instead the virtual programming should augment and accentuate the learning already occurring within the classroom and curriculum.

Researcher Jeremy Bailenson (2016) of Stanford University's Virtual Human Interaction Lab identified four "compelling reasons" for using VR technology to reach learning goals. These reasons are (1) when the situation would be otherwise cost-prohibitive, (2) when the scenario is impossible through other means, (3) if the situation would be too dangerous, or (4) if the scenario is counterproductive.

VR technologies provide students the opportunity to travel to locations that would be logistically or physically impossible. Rather than simply looking at a photograph or video of the location, students can experience the space with their full body through the VR module. For instance, they can virtually visit an art museum that is physically across the world, removing the cost and time of travel (reason 1). Virtual reality programs and interactive communities can also be an opportunity for homeschooled students to expand their curriculum. It provides a place for these learners to connect with other students who do not have to be in their local, physical neighborhood. Students can also take other field trips to remote geographical locations that might otherwise be difficult for them to reach. Physically impossible locations also become available: science classes can travel to the microscopic landscape, tour the interior of the human body, or travel within outer space (reason 2). In social studies, students can travel back in time to historical locations or visit a contemporary refugee camp. Taking a social studies class to a virtual warfront is an example of a situation that would otherwise be too dangerous for them to explore in person (reason 3). In a science class, students could immerse themselves in a virtual laboratory, where they can mix dangerous chemicals and see the resulting chemical reactions. Lastly, VR environments can model counterproductive scenarios, such as deforestation or overfishing, to help students understand the consequences of these actions on the ecosystem without causing environmental destruction.

Another place where VR technologies are useful for K–12 classes is where a 3D model is superior to a 2D representation. For example, students can get a better understanding of electrons moving among atomic orbitals in a 3D immersive space. The 2D representations of atomic orbitals on a textbook page do not accurately represent the orbitals (Reich 2021). Students studying architecture or physics could interact with elements of a bridge to find areas of stress or tension. In physics, students could construct and run roller coasters to explore the influence of gravity (K-12 Blueprint 2017). In biology classes, conscientious objectors can complete dissections on virtual frogs or fetal pigs. Fashion students can create clothing designs that use outlandish materials that the school could not otherwise provide. In extracurricular programs, coaches and students can use VR to "assess or train team ball sports skills" (Faure et al. 2020). Virtual training programs are already being used in professional sports, like Major League Baseball (MLB) organizations, and college-level NCAA baseball and softball teams (Cohen 2022). Unlike real-world practice, VR training can "control and standardi[z]e situations" and repeatedly perform specific drills that would be too complex to repeat identically on the field (Faure et al. 2020).

Educators are also researching how AR/VR technologies can help students with different learning styles or social and emotional needs. For instance, students on the autism spectrum are practicing everyday visits and social skills in VR modules that model a school experience or a neighborhood street. The VR modules allow them to practice sensory experiences and daily independent living skills through exposure therapies. For the school-based VR module, students might have the opportunity to walk through hallways, talk to classmates, or interact with a teacher. Depending on how the student interacts with an avatar, the avatars might prolong or cut off the social interactions. Students can repeat the scenario as necessary to test different engagement strategies or social skills they are practicing. In the neighborhood street VR module, students can experience the sounds, cars, and street furniture of a busy neighborhood in a safe, virtual environment. Students can also practice safety strategies in an environment that will not cause physical harm (given a secure VR space and not being prone to motion sickness). In all cases, the students can repeat the experience to acclimatize to the environment, practicing the exposure before experiencing the classroom or street scenario firsthand. Researchers have also run exposure therapy with participants with autism who have a phobia of small animals. Both VR and AR therapies had "comparable efficacy" with real-world exposure (Suso-Ribera et al. 2019). VR tools can also give individuals exposure to their phobias in a safe, controlled environment. VR simulation exposure therapies have been applied effectively to adult participants with fear of flying and fear of spiders since the early 2000s (Botella et al. 2004; Garcia-Palacios et al. 2002). However, some research indicates that exposure therapies designed for adults are less effective on children (Bouchard 2011).

In another instance of immersive VR, reading modules like the Microsoft Immersive Reader allow students to focus and block out other distractions. The screen will only display the designated text. The Immersive Reader program can also read the text aloud, highlight each spoken word, indicate syllables or parts of speech, and provide visual and verbal definitions for each word. This immersive technology can support students with their independent reading in a way that is both interactive and stimulating (Zimmerman 2022).

Throughout these VR modules, students are able to practice life skills at their own pace. They can personalize their learning based on the VR mod ules they choose to use. Students can also decide how they wish to explore the virtual environment. Additionally, they can customize the viewing settings within the VR program. Depending on the type of VR module, they could also experience the space in their own language, which can be especially engaging for students who are learning in a setting that is not adapted for their native language. They can then focus entirely on the VR experience without also simultaneously translating the novel verbal information (Lynch 2021).

CONCLUSION

There are many use cases for AR/VR in a variety of educational settings that span from public libraries to K–12 schools to higher education and professional research. As one considers the integration of emerging technologies into their suite of services or the curriculum, careful consideration should be given to the pros and cons of incorporating these resources into the organizational workflow. Research supports the positive effects of incorporating AR/VR into classes. AR/VR-based work has been shown to increase student engagement, while improving psychomotor and cognitive skills (Andersen et al. 2016). AR/VR is also seen as a beneficial tool for equality and inclusiveness in education. For instance, for those on the autism spectrum, VR applications allow them to prepare for social situations that might otherwise make them anxious, such as public speaking or crowds (Jarrold et al. 2013). Alternatively, VR can foster empathy and understanding by allowing a neuro-typical individual the opportunity to experience the world through the eyes of a neuro-divergent person (Rogers 2019). AR/VR also makes certain experiences accessible to those who may not physically be able to participate. Libraries and museums are making collections and exhibits that are often closed off behind glass partitions or located in the archives a sensory experience through emerging technologies in order to enhance learning. One such example is a project at the University of Southern California, where a collaboration between USC Special Collections, the School of Religion and the Archaeology program is creating an immersive, interactive experience focused on a fifteenth-century illuminated manuscript. Using digital photography and 3D modeling they are enabling users to engage with the contents of the manuscript while gaining appreciation for rare materials (USC Dana and David Dornsife College of Letters, Arts and Sciences).

In general, AR/VR in learning activities allows for a constructivist approach to learning (Pavlin and Sužnjević 2019). Constructivism in the classroom encourages active learning where students are in control of their own learning and apply their knowledge. In the case of Georgia Tech's library research class, students participated in group-based work with AR/VR that focused on real-world problems and had them tackle the associated technical challenges as they occurred. Library instructors acted more in the role of advisors and facilitators than the traditional role of "sage on the stage." Students developed their own objectives and goals for the semester in cooperation with the library instructors. This model could be applied in numerous settings, not just higher education. In a K–12 environment at the Mount Vernon School, students begin their immersive technology experience from learning the basics of running code, creating 3D models, and animating them in different kinds of software. The foundational class offers a broad content base in order to help students find their interests as they progress to additional classes in the immersive technology sequence. Once they have a baseline of knowledge and have identified their interests, students can develop personalized projects while working within open-ended project constraints (project prompts) given by the instructor. As with the higher education programs, K–12 instructors can continue supporting each student's projects with feedback and guidance.

In addition to all the positive qualities, some negatives related to emerging technology in education have been noted, such as some users of VR devices experiencing motion sickness while in a virtual environment (Velev and Zlateva 2017). There is also the potential to run into objects within their physical space while wearing the headset. Other negatives involve the cost and the learning curve to adopt some of these technologies, along with the rapidly changing requirements of supporting them. When considering integrating these technologies into your program, it will be important to weigh potential positive outcomes along with any expected hurdles.

AR/VR can provide K–12 educators with interactive tools for learning. These include collections of immersive content and tools for users with learning disabilities. In higher education, AR/VR can help learners understand abstract concepts and apply hands-on experience in low-risk virtual settings. These methods are especially beneficial in STEM courses and medical simulations, just to name a few (Dick 2021). As we reflect on our course developments and pedagogies, this book can be used as a blueprint for designing your own educational program utilizing these emerging technologies that have such growth potential.

REFERENCES

American Library Association (ALA). 2008. "Mission and priorities." June 9. http://www.ala.org/aboutala/missionpriorities.

Andersen, Steven Arild Wuyts, Peter Trier Mikkelsen, Lars Konge, Per Cayé-Thomasen, and Mads Sølvsten Sørensen. 2016. "Cognitive load in mastoidectomy skills training: Virtual reality simulation and traditional dissection compared." *Journal of Surgical Education* 73 (1): 45–50. https://doi.org/10.1016/j.jsurg.2015.09.010.

Bailenson, Jeremy. 2016. "The trials and tribulations of narrative in VR." *MediaX Stanford*. November 16, 2016. Video, 17:42. https://www.youtube.com/watch?v=mF78lwAKrRw.

Botella, Cristina, J. Osma, Azucena García-Palacios, Soledad Quero, and Rosa M. Baños. 2004. "Treatment of flying phobia using virtual reality: Data from a 1-year follow-up using a multiple baseline design." *Clinical Psychology & Psychotherapy* 11 (5): 311–323. https://doi.org/10.1002/cpp.404.

Bouchard, Stéphane. 2011. "Could virtual reality be effective in treating children with phobias?" *Expert Review of Neurotherapeutics* 11 (2): 207–213. https://doi.org/10.1586/ern.10.196.

Clatworthy, Keith. n.d. "Visual reference." 20th century stereo viewers. https://www.viewmaster.co.uk/htm/quickref.asp.

Cohen, Andrew. 2022. "WIN reality's VR hitting ads featuring CC Sabathia to air during MLB games on ESPN, TBS, Fox." *SportTechie*, June 6. https://www.sporttechie.com/win-realitys-vr-hitting-ads-featuring-cc-sabathia-to-air-during-mlb-games-on-espn-tbs-fox/.

Craig, Emory, and Maya Georgieva. 2017. "AR and VR in STEM: The new frontiers in science." *Educause Review*. August 4. https://er.educause.edu/blogs/2017/8/ar-and-vr-in-stem-the-new-frontiers-in-science.

CTD Institute. 2018. "Virtual reality and assistive technology: Learn about the new things!" July 25. https://www.ctdinstitute.org/library/2018-07-25/virtual-reality-and-assistive-technology-learn-about-new-new-things.

Dick, Ellysse. 2021. "The promise of immersive learning: Augmented and virtual reality's potential in education." *Itif.org*. August 30. https://itif.org/publications/2021/08/30/promise-immersive-learning-augmented-and-virtual-reality-potential/.

Faure, Charles, Annabelle Limballe, Benoit Bideau, and Richard Kulpa. 2020. "Virtual reality to assess and train team ball sports performance: A scoping review." *Journal of Sports Sciences* 38 (2): 192–205. https://www.tandfonline.com/doi/abs/10.1080/02640414.2019.1689807.

Garcia-Palacios, Azucena, Hunter G. Hoffman, A. Carlin, T. A. Furness, and Cristina Botella. 2002. "Virtual reality in the treatment of spider phobia: A controlled study." *Behaviour Research and Therapy* 40 (9): 983–993. https://doi.org/10.1016/S0005-7967(01)00068-7.

Georgia Tech Computational Media. n.d. "About computational media." https://cm.lmc.gatech.edu/major-overview/.

Georgia Tech Library. n.d. "retroTECH." https://www.library.gatech.edu/retrotech.

Jacobson, Linda. 2019. "As K-12 virtual reality use grows, researchers consider impact on children." *K-12 Dive*, May 22. k12dive.com/news/as-vr-use-grows-in-k-12-researchers-consider-its-impact-on-children/555085.

Jarrold, William, Peter Mundy, Mary Gwaltney, Jeremy Bailenson, Naomi Hatt, Nancy McIntyre, Kwanguk Kim, Marjorie Solomon, Stephanie Novotny, and Lindsay Swain. 2013. "Social attention in a virtual public speaking task in higher functioning children with autism." *Autism Research* 6 (5): 393–410. https://doi.org/10.1002/aur.1302.

K-12 Blueprint. 2017. "Reality bytes: Virtual reality and K-12 education." *K-12 Blueprint*. https://www.k12blueprint.com/news/reality-bytes-virtual-reality-and-k-12-education.

Kavanagh, Sam, Andrew Luxton-Reilly, Burkhard Wuensche, and Beryl Plimmer. 2017. "A systematic review of virtual reality in education." *Themes in Science and Technology Education* 10 (2): 85–119.

Kubelka, Morgan. 2016. "Partnering for success: Best practices in embedded librarianship." *The Wiley Network*, November 9. https://www.wiley.com/network/librarians/library-impact/partnering-for-success-best-practices-in-embedded-librarianship.

Labster. n.d. "Labster." https://www.labster.com/.

Lynch, Matthew. 2021. "Virtual reality matures in the K-12 classroom." *The Tech Edvocate*, January 5. https://www.thetechedvocate.org/virtual-reality-matures-in-the-k-12-classroom/.

Mount Vernon School. n.d. "Innovation diploma." https://mountvernonschool.org/learning-and-life/innovation-diploma/.

Murray-Rust, C., A. Doshi, J. Forrest, X. Mi, and A. Valk. 2019. Data literacy as a pathway to data science at Georgia Tech. *Research Library Issues* 298: 6–15.

Online Etymology Dictionary. n.d. "virtual (adj.)" https://www.etymonline.com/search?q=virtual.

Patterson, John. 2009. "A history of 3D cinema." *The Guardian*, August 19. https://www.theguardian.com/film/2009/aug/20/3d-film-history.

Pavlin, H. M., and M. Sužnjević. 2019. "The opinions and attitudes of students—Future IT teachers—on the use of VR and AR in teaching." 42nd International Convention on Information and Communication Technology, Electronics and Microelectronics (MIPRO). https://doi.org/10.23919/mipro.2019.8757001.

Peekhaus, Wilhelm. 2018. "Seed libraries: Sowing the seeds for community and public library resilience." *The Library Quarterly* 88 (3): 271–285. https://doi.org/10.1086/697706.

Reich, Henry. 2021. "A better way to picture atoms." *MinutePhysics*. May 19. Video, 5:34. https://youtu.be/W2Xb2GFK2yc.

Rogers, Sol. 2019. "How virtual reality can help those with autism." *Forbes*. https://www.forbes.com/sites/solrogers/2019/04/03/how-virtual-reality-can-help-those-with-autism/?sh=68d7f7f1198e.

Saraniero, Patricia L. 2008. "I teach what I do, I do what I teach: The experiences and impacts of teaching artists." EdD diss., University of San Diego. https://www.researchgate.net/publication/255594150_I_Teach_What_I_Do_I_Do_What_I_Teach_A_Study_of_the_Experiences_and_Impacts_of_Teaching_Artists.

Slayden, Kendall, and Marie Graham. 2018. "Walter Greenleaf, neuroscientist and head of Stanford VR Lab." *ChildArt*, October-December: 24–25.

Suso-Ribera, Carlos, Javier Fernández-Álvarez, Azucena García-Palacios, Hunter G. Hoffman, Juani Bretón-López, Rosa M. Baños, Soledad Quero, and Cristina Botella. 2019. "Virtual reality, augmented reality, and in vivo exposure therapy: A preliminary comparison of treatment efficacy in small animal phobia." *Cyberpsychology, Behavior, and Social Networking* 22 (1): 31–38. http://doi.org/10.1089/cyber.2017.0672.

Thompson, Clive. 2017. "Stereographs were the original virtual reality." *Smithsonian Magazine*. https://www.smithsonianmag.com/innovation/sterographs-original-virtual-reality-180964771/.

Turi, Jon. 2014. "The sights and scents of the Sensorama Simulator." *engadget*, February 16. https://www.engadget.com/2014-02-16-morton-heiligs-sensorama-simulator.html.

"Using virtual reality to explore 15th century illuminated manuscripts > XRLab > USC Dana and David Dornsife College of Letters, Arts and Sciences." n.d. Dornsife.usc.edu. https://dornsife.usc.edu/xrlab/neh-vr-exploration-of-illuminated-manuscripts/.

Valk, Alison. 2019. "Systems thinking and arts integration through library educational programming on a STEM campus." *New Review of Academic Librarianship* 25 (2–4): 244–270. https://doi.org/10.1080/13614533.2019.1623271.

Velev, Dimiter, and Plamena Zlateva. 2017. "Virtual reality challenges in education and training." *International Journal of Learning and Teaching* 3 (1). https://doi.org/10.18178/ijlt.3.1.33-37.

Zimmerman, Eli. 2022. "AR/VR in K–12: Schools use immersive technology for assistive learning." *EdTech Magazine*, August 22. https://edtechmagazine.com/k12/article/2019/08/arvr-k-12-schools-use-immersive-technology-assistive-learning-perfcon.

TWO

Getting Started Where You Are: Needs Assessments and Resource Evaluation

Service development and educational programming need to be aligned with the institution's vision and strategic goals. Before starting an AR/VR program or integrating technology with your instructional goals, the initiators of this work need to first consider the institution or school's values or vision statement, both explicit and implicit. Student learning can be tied to the organization's larger strategic goals. If your new program can be directly connected to the school's strategic goals, you might gain greater administrative buy-in and promotion from multiple stakeholders. There might also be more institutional resources available to you such as internal grants. It will be important to ask yourself questions such as: What are the current goals or specialties of your institution? Can you link your project ideas to the larger vision of your department or organization?

As you consider the school or institution itself, also think of the unique aspects in your organization's environment:

- What are the specific areas of research or study?
- Is there a unique local ecosystem?
- Are there any specific student learning profiles, notable alumni?
- Are there unique local communities that frequently collaborate with your organization?

These organizational characteristics can help enhance or complement an educational program that leverages AR/VR and other emerging technologies.

Having aligned your program ideas to the institution's vision and strategic goals, the next step is to discover how emerging technologies can enhance or enrich your existing curriculum. What are you already teaching that could benefit from the affordances mentioned in Chapter 1? These affordances include user presence, user embodiment, and situations that are otherwise dangerous, costly, impossible, or less productive. The gaps on these affordances provide learning opportunities for technologies using AR and VR.

EVALUATING ORGANIZATIONAL GOALS AND COMMUNITY INTERESTS

For libraries and educational organizations that are considering starting an AR/VR program, the choices and possibilities can seem overwhelming. One way to start this process that the authors practiced and found helpful is to evaluate the local environment and the available resources right where you are. An environmental scan to evaluate institutional programs, student interests, technological infrastructure, and financial resources can guide you to a starting point. For instance, what ideas are you, your team, your students, and your institution interested in pursuing? It's likely you are going to be spending a lot of time with this project, so it's useful to consider not only what is technically possible but what your stakeholders are interested in! Understanding your local environment can help you develop a realistic framework for your organization and set the program up for success.

Review worksheets at the end of Chapter 2 for a simplified checklist on the key components to consider as you complete your resource assessments and evaluations.

Before beginning on this endeavor, it may be worth asking yourself what is driving this initiative and whether you will have any major limitations because of your current technology infrastructure. In other words, what will have the greatest impact on your service design: community interests or technology?

Information collection methods for consideration may include environmental scans, surveys, focus groups, small-scale pilots, and administrator feedback. Each of these methods offer a particular process of strategic information gathering.

1. An environmental scan is "the identification and monitoring of factors from both inside and outside the organization that may impact the long-term viability of the organization," or in this context, the service (Fordham University, n.d.; Washington State DOH 2011).
2. Online or paper surveys collect information from stakeholders about their interests, opinions, and preferences. Online services like SurveyMonkey, TypeForm, or GoogleForms offer ways to customize, disseminate, and review survey feedback. While using surveys, it is important to keep in mind that most online surveys receive only a 10–30 percent response rate (Qualtrics, n.d.).
3. The phrase "focus group" might be used informally to describe gathering a small group of people to discuss an issue, product, or plan. However, the term specifically refers to a "carefully planned series of discussions designed to obtain perceptions on a defined area of interest in a permissive, non-threatening environment" (Iowa State University Extension 2004).
4. A pilot program or feasibility study "is a small-scale, short-term experiment that helps an organization learn how a large-scale project might work in practice." It is an excellent way to get a sense of logistical challenges before embarking on a large-scale project (Search CIO, n.d.).
5. Lastly, asking administrators for feedback can give service managers an idea of what the organization's leadership is prioritizing. It helps the service managers project and plan resources and support and adjust the expectation and tone of your future project pitches.

Environmental Scan in Higher Ed

For the Georgia Tech Library, beginning the AR/VR program was a twofold process. The library focused on both the goals of the institute and then the needs of the students. First, the library's mission and vision states "The Georgia Tech Library defines excellence in the creation, preservation, curation, and connection of scholarship. Through this work we create new paths of learning, knowledge, information, and resources to develop leaders who advance technology and improve the human condition" (Georgia Tech Library, n.d.). At Georgia Tech, research, including student research, is often interdisciplinary. Librarians are trained to work closely with researchers and identify synergies across campus. Building on the strategic vision of the organization, the librarian team was able to identify areas of research on campus that aligned with emerging technologies (AR/VR). The librarians regularly scan through the curriculum gap and devise solutions that integrate emerging technologies to meet students' needs. A scan of the course offerings on campus in 2017–2018 showed that there were very few classes with topics such as computer vision, computer graphics, or video game design tied to extended reality (XR) technologies. For those that did, they either focused on specific research topics or were only open to specific programs. Most of these courses emphasized the theoretical or mathematical aspects of computing.

After close analysis of the school's current program of study, the team connected with key individuals within the institution directly involved in curriculum development and student advising. Two programs stood out. The computational media program provides students with both hands-on and theoretical knowledge of computing, as well as an understanding of visual design and the history of media (Georgia Institute of Technology, n.d.b). The College of Computing provides an intellectual home for centers devoted to both practical and theoretical application in areas from hardware systems and information security to robotics and human–computer interaction (Georgia Institute of Technology, n.d.c). These programs of study have a framework in place that allows select students within those schools to collaborate with faculty and researchers on individualized research. The student-driven research provides a benefit to both the student and the faculty on campus. Students receive credit for their work as well as practical experience, and faculty gain additional insight into the area of the research by partnering with the students. As a result, Georgia Tech librarians leveraged this existing framework to develop a research section that engages students and explores the use of AR/VR for teaching and learning through the lens of a library environment. The Georgia Tech Library embarked on a research partnership with students who were awarded academic credit for their efforts. One of the long-term goals of this educational initiative was to expand these AR/VR research opportunities to students from multiple disciplines and majors across campus, thus making the technology more accessible.

Environmental Scan in K–12 Schools

Mount Vernon School in Atlanta, Georgia, has a "national reputation for exploring, discovering, asking, and risking" exemplified in their existing upper school Maker, Design & Engineering Program, along with an Innovation Diploma Program (Toller 2018). This institutional spirit led to its exploration of the potential of utilizing VR in students learning. The students have also shown interest in immersive technology, especially as they were pursuing technological projects in the student-led design studio even before the school developed the VR Lab. Additionally, a group of students paired with their immersive technology teacher to contact Dell/Alienware in order to partner with the company to build out the Mount Vernon VR Lab (Toller 2018).

In the process of exploring VR for teaching and learning, educators at Mount Vernon connect to colleagues across departments to share information and resources. For example, a lower school educator could connect with colleagues in the middle school, which already had a 360 camera. The lower school educator could bring this camera to younger students as they created an immersive video in collaboration with the school's Admissions Department.

MATCHING STUDENT AND STAKEHOLDER SKILLS AND INTERESTS

When developing new programming, it is critical to consider stakeholders' interests. Stakeholders can vary depending on your environment, including but not limited to educators, researchers, students, technology specialists, administrators, artists, sponsors, or community members, just to name a few.

> *See the resources at the end of the chapter for tips on completing a stakeholder analysis in an educational setting.*

Finding the concepts and causes students are passionate about can help sustain interest and engagement through any of the hurdles and challenges of learning a new technology. Additionally, discovering what fellow educators are interested in may lead to mutual interests that can lead to cross-curricular programming, thus drawing on the strengths of both disciplines. An organization should consider nontraditional partnerships; for instance, bringing together computer science educators, art teachers, or theater teachers to offer diverse learning options in conjunction with these fields. Nonacademic groups such as student clubs or student organizations can be partners in programming. Other partners to consider while developing services include IT professionals and administrative support. Community members and occasionally sponsors can step in to offer project ideas. These ideas could be synthesized to inspire programming initiatives such as an XR hackathon.

In addition to assessing student interests, it's also useful to identify their skills. This might be a questionnaire that you issue to students at the beginning of a class, or a questionnaire you issue to the student body in general (e.g., through a school newsletter, assembly, or existing art/science/computer class). These questions help determine what skills students already have and what tools they might already know how to use (smartphones, C++ or C#, Unity, Unreal Engine, video editing, 3D modeling, photography, or others). This questionnaire can also cover what types of technology students are interested in pursuing, such as AR, VR, other emerging technology, using preexisting content, or creating their own experiences. Knowledge of student skills and interests can help instructors and librarians tailor the learning activities within a course toward helping students develop a skillset that enables them to create their own original concepts and meet self-defined goals.

Student Skills and Interests in Higher Ed

Through the environmental scan of emerging technologies at Georgia Tech, the librarians discovered the potential to design a low-stakes, nonlecture, hands-on development course for students to gain firsthand VR development experience.

To provide a course environment with a realistic time commitment, the program allows students to register for one, two, or three credits as they see fit. Beginning in the fall of 2018, this librarian-led VR session was listed in the campus class catalog as one of the undergraduate research sections available to students in the computational media program. To get started with the class, the librarians had two challenges to address: limited VR resources and varying skill levels among the cohort of students. One approach to addressing these challenges is to maximize the use of free resources available on campus and online. Thus, leveraging any open-source tools was key to accommodating student projects. This course was designed as one in which students propose their own projects. To assess if the student objectives were realistic, the librarians designed an intake form that students complete first. This survey gathered information to understand students' previous VR experience and any project ideas they have in mind. A view of students' technical backgrounds and interests helps instructors estimate the level and scope of the projects that they can realistically complete within a semester. This process allows the instructors and students to work together effectively on the project design. Second, the research team would search available resources in the library, on campus, and online for project implementation.

Due to its hands-on nature, this research section requires intense coding and debugging. It is the instructors' belief that a big motivator toward completing the bulk of these projects is students' passion for telling their stories through VR technologies. So, it is critical that the students be invested in their project proposal. The librarians leading this class focus on connecting the students' project ideas to personal interests. Therefore, it is important for students to have control over what stories they choose to tell. The project ideas are by no means a commitment; students are always allowed, and in many cases encouraged, to adjust the design over the course of the semester to make sure the workloads are manageable.

See the resources at the end of the chapter for example questions included on the Georgia Tech questionnaire and self-assessment.

Student Skills and Interests in K–12 Schools

An upper school educator at the Galloway School in Atlanta, Georgia, was inspired to bring an immersive media experience back to her students after seeing a botany AR demonstration at a conference. Students in semester-long Animation and Mixed Realities classes were very interested in using immersive tools to address the ecological problems of species extinction and natural resource depletion. They used Sketch Fab to generate 3D models of plants and animals, along with the Merge Cube app and an AR development app on the iPad. The Merge Cube app, which uses QR Designs to activate AR experiences on a smartphone or iPod Touch, was a great match for introducing students to the emerging technologies. Plus, the Merge Cubes are inexpensive and work with smartphones, which are readily available to students. The project was comparatively fast, and students from around the school, not just the class, could interact with the technology.

The educators then planned a cross-curricular J-Term Excursion, which is a short-term class offered in January or February between the normal fall and spring semesters. This particular J-Term Excursion was a partnership among biology, art, and technology teachers in the format of a 10-day trip. Teachers took a group of students to the Galapagos Islands to record the ecological environment. Students kept sketchbooks, used a 360 camera, and created augmented reality content to engage viewers in the unique Galapagos ecosystem. Having an educational experience in between semesters during this alternative time range gave students interested in biology or visual art the chance to experience VR curriculum outside of their regular classes. The alternative time also allowed the instructors to create a curriculum more flexible and more specialized than a semester-long course.

EVALUATING TECHNOLOGY

In addition to assessing the needs of your students and the strategic goals of the organization, another early step is to evaluate your current technology infrastructure and assess the channels for acquiring more resources. One method for understanding more about an organization's state of readiness regarding technology programs is to perform a SWOT (strengths, weaknesses, opportunities, threats) analysis. A SWOT analysis will assist in identifying the current internal strengths and weaknesses that can create opportunities and threats for an organization. Using this analysis technique will allow you to leverage existing strengths in your organization while avoiding or addressing challenges that may prevent you from reaching your strategic goals. Evaluating technology or performing a technology SWOT analysis should be a collaborative endeavor between educators and information technology professionals. Additional questions to answer that will guide decisions:

1. What learning outcomes best match your curriculum goals?
2. What content will students be creating? Will students be using preexisting assets or creating their own content?
3. Review your current budget. Are there any limitations?

A first step can be taking an inventory of the types of computers, tablets, hardware, and software that your school already has. Ensure that the goals for your new program or class align with the technology infrastructure your organization has in place. Finding resources that are compatible with existing technology can leverage materials you already have access to. For instance, instead of purchasing an independent 3D scanning machine, students could use an iPad app for 3D scanning as the program begins. Keep in mind the development environment required for AR/VR is resource intensive; computers used for this purpose have high requirements for processing power and graphics cards. Additionally, take an inventory on your existing power and data ports.

Second, consider the survey responses from students for their interests and skill levels when acquiring new technologies. If students are more interested in augmented reality the learning curve is much less steep and resources are easier to acquire. Additionally, what are the time constraints on this project? How old are the students ? Identify their skill levels, coordination levels, and if there are any age-based guidelines on software use or screen time limits. How many students will be working together in the class? All of these elements can inform the technology you purchase. For instance, you might purchase one high-level heavy-duty VR headset, with coordinating hand-controllers, or, instead, a few lightweight "cardboard" VR headsets that work in conjunction with smartphones and do not have hand-controllers. Identify other teachers, departments, or technology specialists who are willing to discuss the feasibility of your project ideas and provide feedback.

As you select your ideal collection of technology, identify how your school makes educational technology decisions and selections. Will you need someone to approve this project or purchase? An IT department might oversee acquisition of classroom technology tools and provide tech support. In other cases, it might be you that provides the tech support for these projects! Chapter 3 will include more information about technology lending programs, inventory control, and securing your technology assets.

With a good understanding of the organization's existing technologies, tools needed, and the available budget, the librarians/instructors can define service expectations and outline classroom requirements for the current year and update plans for future years. This is an iterative process; service managers should develop a system for continuously assessing technologies. It will be important to develop a long-life loose fit for your initiatives, as technology changes rapidly.

Evaluating Technology in Higher Ed

Critical to Georgia Tech's technology selection process is backward design. Backward design is a course design process that begins with instructors identifying student learning goals and then designing course content and assessments to help students achieve these goals (Center for Teaching and Learning, n.d.). Georgia Tech has a base collection of devices and technology to support AR/VR initiatives that is available to anyone on campus. Students are invited to play games and experiment with this collection of resources in designated spaces in the library; or if the device is untethered, they are welcome to take it with them anywhere. After gaining some familiarity with the technology, students participating in the library's research class craft detailed proposals along with a self-assessment on their current skills. Driven largely by the self-assessments and proposals, the instructors map out what additional resources are needed to help the students achieve their goals while also providing a realistic framework for the finite time available in the semester. Central to this approach are play-based educational methods, providing students with a low-stakes environment to experiment with the technologies and foster engagement and creativity. As noted by James and Nerantzi, play can bring together cognitive, emotional, and psychomotor elements of learning, making learning more relatable and a more holistic experience (2019).

The process for evaluating technology at the Georgia Tech library both on micro and macro level mirrors the LEAPS (learner analysis, engagement, accessibility, purpose of instruction, and sustainability) framework as described by Laura Lohman. First, through learner analysis (Lohman 2021) we look at the students' initial skills, attitude, experience, and overall learning goals. "Thoughtful learner analysis generates observations about the diversity of learners and undergirds selection of digital technologies that can support inclusive learning environments" (Lohman 2021). Since the research course is designed to be a collaborative research project between students and the library, many of the tasks associated with the work are team-based. Therefore, potential for engagement is also a major factor in technology selection. For instance, students need tools that allow them to collaboratively work on 3D models. Students who choose to use the free open-source tool of Blender for 3D modeling can add extensions or plugs-in to the software that allow multiple users to work on the same scene or model in real time. Accessibility is another important building block in the technology selection process. In order to create an inclusive environment, technologies should be made available to students who require them. Georgia Tech Library's AR/VR collection development follows the industry recommendation to go untethered. This allows users to use devices anywhere as stand-alone. For the legacy devices that are still tethered, the library provides a designated room with workstation and an associated account to allow students access to the development environment. As noted earlier, the technology you select should be rooted in the learning objectives of the class and on a larger scale the goals of your institution.

Mapping technology selections to the learning objectives and the student goals will also contribute to effective assessment. If the educational objective of a class is to learn about a particular location and students are creating a virtual tour to orient and educate users about this location, it would be critical to make technology selections that support the initial learning objective. These selections can also translate to professional skills students will use beyond their college experience. In this particular example, instructors may want to familiarize students with technologies frequently used in the real estate industry for virtual tours, such as 360 cameras.

Finally, the librarians looked at both pedagogical longevity and technological longevity. Sustainability can affect how often your course content will need to be refreshed or how often you may have to purchase new software. There are pros and cons to almost all scenarios. With certain open-source software or apps you may find your team asking how often is the software maintained? Software or apps that are abandoned and no longer updated by developers may no longer be a reliable resource. The software you select to utilize could even be purchased by a company that then makes this a tool you have to pay for, which could be an unexpected expense. If you choose a resource that is cost prohibitive, will you be able to keep it up in the long term? Planning for the long term and choosing tools that allow you to pivot quickly when needed will create an environment that is easier for educators to manage.

Ultimately, none of these decisions are made in a vacuum. For Georgia Tech, we are actively engaged with our IT support team. Creating a culture of shared communication and ongoing dialogue about best practices and trends in educational technology will assist in fostering student learning.

> *Review LEAPS concepts in the resources section at the end of the chapter for the five factors: learner analysis, engagement, accessibility, purpose of instruction, and sustainability.*
>
> *See a list of resources for current edtech trends at the end of the chapter.*

Evaluating Technology Needs in K–12 Schools

In Mount Vernon's upper school immersive technology program, instructors selected design engines and coding languages that would be less intense for students to use in their first projects. For example, students are encouraged to begin with preexisting assets, learning how to work with the models in the design and interactive phases, before creating 3D models themselves. When it comes to the game engine students use to create their projects, the school picks the open-source game engine Unity. The reason the school chose Unity is because it offers detailed hands-on tutorials that students can follow in conjunction with class lectures.

K–12 school students have grown up in a different time technologically compared to the instructors. Technology hardware and software are usually selected by instructors, and so students will need assistance adapting to the technology. Some students may already have experience using the hardware or software, while others will be new to the experience. In either case, it's helpful for students to learn the instructor's expectations for interacting with the technology in an educational setting. As instructors introduce them to the hardware options, it can be useful to start with basic training. For instance, some younger students might be more familiar with the input technologies of track pads and touch screens and will thus need specific instruction on how to effectively use a separate computer mouse to navigate a computer station. Students may also need reminders about how to organize, name, save, and manage files in formats or arrangements that are most conducive to the particular software or hardware they are using.

ACCESSIBILITY ACCOMMODATIONS AND OPPORTUNITIES

When it comes to developing learning resources, accessibility and inclusion are key to a successful experience. AR/VR/MR services should focus on making the devices and use of them accessible and inclusive to all that need to use them. Therefore, accessibility should be part of the design of technology selections and solutions. All learners can benefit from a welcoming technology setup that takes into consideration the needs of participants of different ages or language backgrounds, those who have motor disabilities or are deaf or hard of hearing or in chronic pain, and those who have low vision or wear corrective lenses.

National compliance and international guidelines call for technology and information accessibility. In the United States, Section 508 legislation "requires that the federal government procure, create, use and maintain ICT [information and communications technology] that is accessible to people with disabilities, regardless of whether or not they work for the federal government" (U.S. EPA, 2022). The U.S. Department of Health and

Human Services offers accessibility checklists for older forms of technology that must be compliant (U.S. HHS 2021). The international community of the World Wide Web Consortium (W3C) has created Web Content Accessibility Guidelines (WCAG) 2.0 and 2.1, which includes standards for developing and maintaining a Web that is accessible to the broadest array of users. The W3C goes into more detail about adaptation for virtual reality in a separate document, including a variety of considerations that are appropriate to our discussions (W3C 2017). First, VR environments offer alternative modes of interaction for users standing or sitting, ways of manipulating controllers, and the expectations for range of motion (including alternatives to big movements, reaching, or using a button to open a virtual door instead of mimicking the broad motion of opening a door). Since the environment is virtual, it could "be modified to address access needs in ways that the real environment, in general, cannot be" (W3C 2017), giving people with physical limitations access to the experience that they would not have otherwise. Two examples from Microsoft include SeeingVR, which are engine plugins for Unity that offer "14 tools to tackle visual impairment challenges" and the "canetroller" that "works as a white cane but integrates into the virtual reality environment" providing auditory and haptic feedback to the user (VanFossen 2019). Second, VR environments give users the opportunity to use text-to-speech resources or to adjust visual settings, including menus, screen resolution, button placement, and screen contrast. This is critical to visually impaired users. Third, VR device manufacturers and content makers can respond to longer-term considerations of comfort and usability, including headset or controller weight, which has already been improved from VIVE to Oculus Quest, accommodating user body proportions, and the mechanics of using a headset over glasses or different hairstyles (Formaker-Olivas 2019).

Accessibility and inclusion in the context of AR/VR technologies include not only the device availability, but also the setup. A good resource to use to assess accessibility and inclusiveness of educational technology is the checklists and resources provided by the Center for Universal Design in Education at the University of Washington through their disabilities, opportunities, internetworking, and technology program. Of particular relevance to our topics are some of the accommodations they suggest for computer labs and software setups including adjustable-height tables, screen readers, screen enlargement software or large monitors, work areas for left- and right-handed users, and controls that can be reached from a seated position (Access Computing 2018).

As mentioned in Chapter 1, VR resources can also be used to share disability experiences with learners who do not have those same challenges. Lessons like those from Amanda Licastro, Eric Baratta, and David Toccafondi at the Digital Library Federation (DLF) Digital Library Pedagogy Working Group share strategies to scaffold and support students exploring a variety of VR environments (Licastro, Baratta and Toccafondi 2021). The VR lessons here cover blindness, hearing loss, autism, and depression.

EVALUATING BUDGET AND FINANCIAL NEEDS

Access to up-to-date headsets, AR/VR hardware and software, as well as needed support means spending. Limits on an organization's budget can discourage administrators from wanting to make a financial commitment. Many resources such as software have ongoing costs associated with them. To minimize the challenges associated with budget constraints, we recommend starting small, with only a few devices to address the existing community needs. One approach that could maximize the use of a limited number of VR devices might be a pilot program for your community members with short-term commitments. Depending on your organization's budget, program architects may need to identify any internal grants your school offers or external grants that your institution may be eligible for.

While writing the proposal and planning your program, consider the timeline for writing, submitting, and enacting the grant, given that you are awarded the funds. If you are approaching an administrator, consider some of the following key points and adjust them to best fit your circumstances. Your presentation could identify how the integration of emerging technology ties into the school's vision, values, initiatives; how many students this project could potentially reach; the learning outcomes and additional benefits to students through the unique affordances of VR; how the project will use existing school capital and resources; partnerships with other community resources or corporations; the price per student; and how you have considered cost-sharing options, including internal and external grants and school-year timing.

Budgeting in Higher Ed

Most organizations have a base budget to work with; Georgia Tech is no exception. The AR/VR resources at Georgia Tech are largely funded by student technology fees and the library's technology funds.

Beyond base resources, the library leverages partnerships with departments on campus to acquire new tools. In most cases, additional funding for emerging technology in libraries and school environments are coming from both internal and external grant opportunities (Varnum 2019). At Georgia Tech, the Institute for People and Technology (IPAT) provides the annual Research and Engagement grant. The goal of these grants is to foster interdisciplinary collaborations and research with a focus on community engagement. Awardees present brown bag panels and a final report to the larger campus community at the conclusion of the semester. These grants are often awarded as seed grants to projects that have the potential to lead to extramural funding in the future (Georgia Institute of Technology IPAT, n.d.). There are also external grants to look at. Georgia Tech's team utilized resources such as PIVOT to locate appropriate opportunities. PIVOT is global source of funding opportunities. The tool allows you to save searches, define criteria, and manage alerts for new grants (PIVOT, n.d.). There are also a variety of grants by the Institute of Museum and Library Services that offer opportunities for tying these immersive technologies to specific learning goals or communities.

Real-World Experiences in K–12 Schools

The Galloway School also offers an internal Innovation grant that resembles Georgia Tech's internal grant opportunities. One year Galloway's grant program allowed immersive technology educators to purchase special VR products to use in conjunction with a donated Oculus Rift headset. The Innovation grant is a proposal-based resource that can be applied to projects that use at least two of the initials in STEAM (science, technology, engineering, arts, and mathematics). The usual grant proposal will be headed by one or two teachers from as many grade levels. A committee of administrators and teachers reviews proposals and decides which ones to approve on a yearly basis.

The internal grant proposals are not restricted solely to faculty. When a group of high school students were working on an independent project in VR, their instructors had them write and assemble the grant proposal. This was an excellent real-world experience for the students to practice composing and promoting their ideas in writing. The students worked with instructors to edit and prepare the proposal for a timely submission to the committee.

Additional Grant-Seeking Information

Even if your institution does not offer internal grants like the examples mentioned, there are numerous grants resources available to libraries and organizations. Some of the grants offered through the Institute of Museum and Library Services (IMLS; https://www.imls.gov/grants/grant-programs) could match AR/VR programming. For all types of libraries, the Community Catalyst initiative supports projects that encourage community engagement (https://www.imls.gov/our-work/priority-areas/community-catalyst-initiative). Higher-ed libraries pursuing AR/VR programs could seek the Digital Humanities Advancement grants (https://www.imls.gov/grants/available/digital-humanities-advancement-grants). These grants "support innovative, experimental, and/or computationally challenging digital projects," whether they are just getting started or if they are long-standing projects.

Additional grants can be found at the federal, state, and local level. As an example, at the federal level, the U.S. Department of Education occasionally offers virtual reality design challenges like the EdSim Challenge, which awarded $680,000 for solutions providing students with the ability to partake in "immersive simulations that transfer academic, technical, and employability skills" (U.S. Department of Education 2017). Other current grants can be searched at the federal grant website http://www.grants.gov.

> *See the resources at the end of the chapter for guides for drafting grant proposals.*

Community organizations like Rotary Clubs or Lions Clubs are sometimes interested in funding programs at local schools and libraries. A STEAM school in North Carolina added a VR "headset with two remote controls and a gaming computer" to their lab with a grant from the community Rotary Club (Schaffhauser 2019). Corporate matches, corporate grants, or local company partnerships can also provide funding to AR/VR programming. For example, a school in Youngsville, Louisiana, partnered with Cargill "to purchase two classroom sets of virtual reality and augmented reality technology" (Guidry 2020). Another school in Tulsa, Oklahoma, partnered with ImaginX to build "an immersive learning lab that uses augmented reality and virtual reality" (Schaffhauser 2020). It can also be worthwhile to reach out to companies with your students for small donations. For instance, some companies will "gift" a piece of equipment to a school in exchange for a mention on the school's website or the company's logo incorporated into promotional materials. The company might also be interested in offering one of their pieces of equipment, like a digital tablet, for free as a prize to students. Simply asking is worth a try!

ONGOING ASSESSMENT AND CYCLIC COURSE DEVELOPMENT

In addition to the initial needs assessments, information gathering, and analysis critical to beginning your pilot program or new classes, ongoing assessment and curriculum calibration during and after your programming starts will allow you to continually meet the student learning goals and the goals of your organization. This continual evaluation will also inform technological decisions and resource selections. Cyclic course design creates a feedback loop that instructors can build from, then revise and restructure their course content when necessary (Figure 2-1).

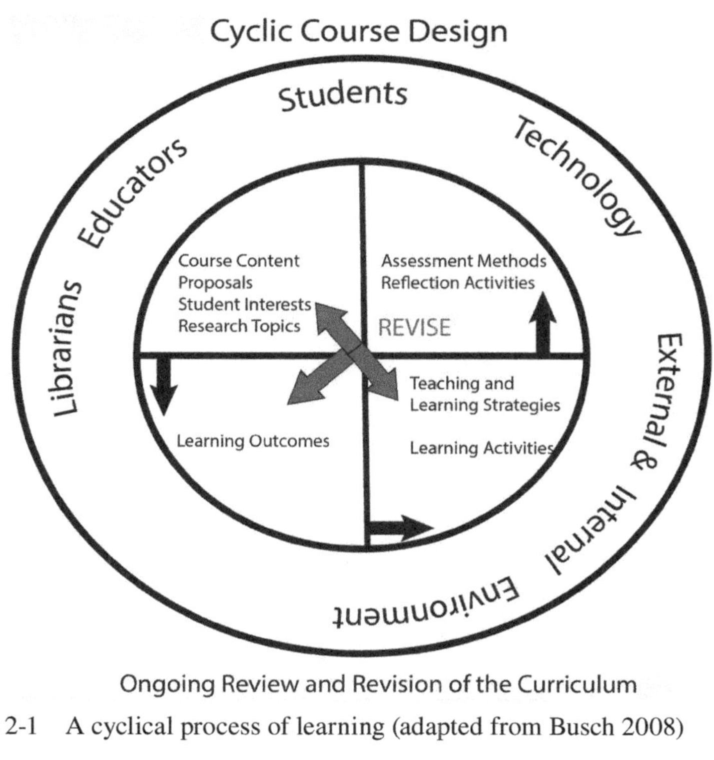

Figure 2-1 A cyclical process of learning (adapted from Busch 2008)

Beginning with the core concepts and the framework of your subject material, instructors can outline student learning objectives through concept maps or mind mapping (Busch 2008). Utilizing Bloom's taxonomy and Gagne's Nine Events of Instruction can also be an effective way to craft initial student learning outcomes and activities. Bloom's taxonomy is a classification system used to define and distinguish different levels of human cognition. There are four levels on the knowledge dimension: factual, conceptual, procedural, and metacognitive. There are six levels on the cognitive process dimension: remembering, understanding, applying, analyzing, evaluating, and creating (Lasley, n.d.). Teaching and learning strategies are developed based on learning objectives. As you design learning activities and student prompts, Gagne's Nine Events can provide you with a framework for engaging activities. Gagne proposed a series of events focused on the mental conditions for learning (Northern Illinois University, 2018). Finally, assessment during the class, through student self-reflections, teaching evaluations, or other metrics inform modifications to course content, learning objectives, or pedagogy. When creating learning activities with AR/VR in mind, utilizing a flexible iterative framework allows you to adjust for multiple variables including the technology and student project concepts.

See more information on crafting learning objectives with Bloom's taxonomy and Gagne's Nine Events in the resources section at the end of the chapter.

REFERENCES

Access Computing. 2018. "Equal access: Universal design of computing departments." University of Washington Center for Universal Design in Education. September 17. https://www.washington.edu/doit/equal-access-universal-design-computing-departments.

Busch, Karen V. 2008. "Conclusion: Making learning visible—A cyclical process." The Scholarship of Teaching and Learning at EMU: Vol. 2, Article 11.3, fig. 9–1. http://commons.emich.edu/sotl/vol2/iss1/11.

Center for Teaching and Learning. n.d. "Glossary of pedagogical terms." https://ctl.wustl.edu/resources/glossary-of-pedagogical-terms/.

Fordham University. n.d. "Conducting an environmental scan." https://www.fordham.edu/info/26625/conducting_an_environmental_scan.

Formaker-Olivas, Ben. 2019. "Why VR/AR developers should prioritize accessibility in UX/UI design." June 14. https://aixr.org/insights/why-vr-ar-developers-should-prioritize-accessibility-in-ux-ui-design/.

Georgia Institute of Technology. n.d.a. "About the Georgia Tech Library." https://library.gatech.edu/about.

Georgia Institute of Technology. n.d.b. "Computational media (BS)." https://www.gatech.edu/academics/degrees/bachelors/computational-media-bs.

Georgia Institute of Technology. n.d.c. "College of Computing research centers: Frames of inquiry." https://www.cc.gatech.edu/research-centers-frames-inquiry.

Georgia Institute of Technology IPAT. n.d. "Research and engagement grants for 2021–2022." https://research.gatech.edu/ipat/research-and-engagement-grants-2021-2022.

Guidry, Leigh. 2020. "Southside High School receives $10K from Cargill for virtual reality learning tools." *The Daily Advertiser*, March 8. https://www.theadvertiser.com/story/news/local/education/2020/03/08/southside-high-school-getting-vr-lab-10-k-grant-cargill/4975565002/.

Iowa State University Extension. 2004. "Can you call it a focus group?" May. https://store.extension.iastate.edu/product/6456.

James, Alison, and Chrissi Nerantzi, eds. 2019. *The power of play in higher education*. Cham: Springer International Publishing. https://doi.org/10.1007/978-3-319-95780-7.

Lasley, Thomas J. n.d. "Bloom's taxonomy: Education." *Encyclopedia Britannica*. https://www.britannica.com/topic/Blooms-taxonomy.

Licastro, Amanda, Eric Baratta, and David Toccafondi. 2021. "Exploring virtual reality through the lens of disability." Digital Library Federation (DLF) Digital Library Pedagogy Working Group, July 21. https://dlfteach.pubpub.org/pub/vol2-licastro-exploring-virtual-reality-through-the-lens-of-disability/release/1.

Lohman, Laura. 2021. "The LEAPS framework for selecting digital technologies in online, hybrid, and face-to-face course design." *Currents in Teaching and Learning* 12 (2): 6–19. https://webcdn.worcester.edu/currents-in-teaching-and-learning/wp-content/uploads/sites/65/2022/05/Currents-Volume-12-Issue-02-Spring-2021.pdf.

Northern Illinois University. 2018. "Gagne's Nine Events of Instruction—NIU—Center for Innovative Teaching and Learning." Northern Illinois

University. https://www.niu.edu/citl/resources/guides/instructional-guide/gagnes-nine-events-of-instruction.shtml.

PIVOT. n.d. "Pivot-RP | Pivot-RP." https://pivot.proquest.com/.

Qualtrics. n.d. "How to increase survey response rates." https://www.qualtrics.com/experience-management/research/tools-increase-response-rate/.

Schaffhauser, Dian. 2019. "North Carolina school adds VR headset system for STEAM education." *The Journal*, January 31. https://thejournal.com/articles/2019/01/30/north-carolina-school-adds-vr-headset-system-for-steam-education.aspx.

Schaffhauser, Dian. 2020. "Tulsa high school to set up AR/VR immersive learning lab." *The Journal*, November 5. https://thejournal.com/articles/2020/11/05/tulsa-high-school-to-set-up-arvr-immersive-learning-lab.aspx.

Search CIO. n.d. "Pilot program (pilot study)." techtarget.com/searchcio/definition/pilot-program-pilot-study.

Toller, Allison. 2018. "An inconceivable partnership: Dell said yes." *The Mount Vernon Magazine*, January 11. http://mvmag.pub/2018/01/11/an-inconceivable-partnership/.

U.S. Department of Education. 2017. "EDSIM challenge." Fall. https://www.edsimchallenge.com/.

U.S. EPA. 2022. "What is Section 508?" https://www.epa.gov/accessibility/what-section-508.

U.S. HHS. 2021. "Accessibility compliance checklists." January 21. https://www.hhs.gov/web/section-508/accessibility-checklists/index.html.

VanFossen, Lorelle. 2019. "Accessibility, disabilities, and virtual reality solutions." *Educators in VR*, May 31. https://educatorsinvr.com/2019/05/31/accessibility-disabilities-and-virtual-reality-solutions/.

Varnum, Kenneth J. 2019. *Beyond reality: Augmented, virtual, and mixed reality in the library.* American Library Association.

W3C. 2017. "Accessibility of virtual reality." October 20. https://www.w3.org/WAI/APA/task-forces/research-questions/wiki/Accessibility_of_Virtual_Reality.

Washington State Department of Health. 2011. "Conduct an environmental scan." February 14. https://www.doh.wa.gov/portals/1/documents/mtgs/2011/20110214-pr-pmc-mod-02-14-11swot08.pdf.

RESOURCES

Overall Checklist for Needs Assessment

An environmental scan will help you develop a realistic framework to set your program up for success. Use an environmental scan when you are starting a program from scratch or when you are assessing a program that has already begun. If you are redeveloping an existing program, your environmental scan will incorporate data and assessments from previous runs.

- ❑ Environmental Scan
  - Organization Goals
  - Community Interests
  - Student Interests
- ❑ Technology Inventory
- ❑ Funding Opportunities
- ❑ Accessibility and Accommodations

Evaluating Organization Goals and Community Interests

- What ideas are you, your team, your students, and your institution interested in pursuing?

  ____

  ____

  ____

  ____

  ____

- What are your institution's explicit and implicit Values, Motto, or Vision Statement?

  ____

  ____

  ____

  ____

  ____

- What unique qualities can be found in your school's environment, student body, alumni, or local community?

  ____

  ____

  ____

  ____

  ____

- What parts of your curriculum could benefit from the affordances of VR (e.g., user presence, user embodiment, dangerous, costly, impossible, counterproductive)?

  ____

  ____

  ____

  ____

  ____

- Other curricular questions to consider:
  - What art, science, and computer classes are you already offering?
  - Where might students have space in their schedule for additional electives?
  - Is there space in your existing curriculum for a new project or a completely new class?
  - Can you try a module in an existing class, as a club or after-school program, or during a summer class or Jan-Term intensive?
  - How can you encourage younger students (6th grade, 9th grade) to join the program?

Evaluating Student Interests and Skills

- What are students passionate about?

  ____

  ____

  ____

  ____

  ____

- What partnerships can you build with other faculty or staff? (physical sciences, computer science, art, home education, shop, tech theater, etc.)

- Where can you question students about their interest in such a program? (in class, through a school newsletter, assembly, or at existing art/science/computer class); what tools might they already know how to use (smartphones, C++ or C#, Unity, Unreal Engine, video editing, 3D modeling, photography, etc.).

- Are you interested in having students build their own experiences or use preexisting content?

Initial Questions to Ask Students Interested in Joining a Research Class

- Basic scheduling availability from each student. This information will be shared with everyone participating.
- What skills and talents will you bring to the team or selected track? What skills and talents would you like to develop? Do you have specific products or outputs that you hope to achieve in the course?
- Distinguish between interest and skill using a series of questions like these pictured on the following pages.

Do you generally prefer to work alone or in teams?

- ☐ Alone
- ☐ Teams
- ☐ Fine with either

Are you comfortable with working on a research project that is largely self directed with periodic check-ins?

- ☐ Yes
- ☐ No
- ☐ I'm not sure - I haven't ever done it

In a sentence or two, please let us know what your main areas of interest are or if you have other skills not mentioned above:

Given the information you know about this section so far, do you have any specific areas of interest or project ideas?

Figure 2-2 Student Interest Survey Questions at a Georgia Tech Research Class

Please indicate your level of interest in the following topics:

Not interested at all	Mildly interested		Interested		Very interested	Very interested and skilled in this area
0	1	2		3	4	5

VR (Virtual Reality) development

Educational Technologies

Video editing and production

Graphic Design/Graphics

Designing workshops or events centered around technology

3D scanning

3D modelling

AR (Augmented Reality)

Figure 2-3 More Student Interest Survey Questions at a Georgia Tech Research Class

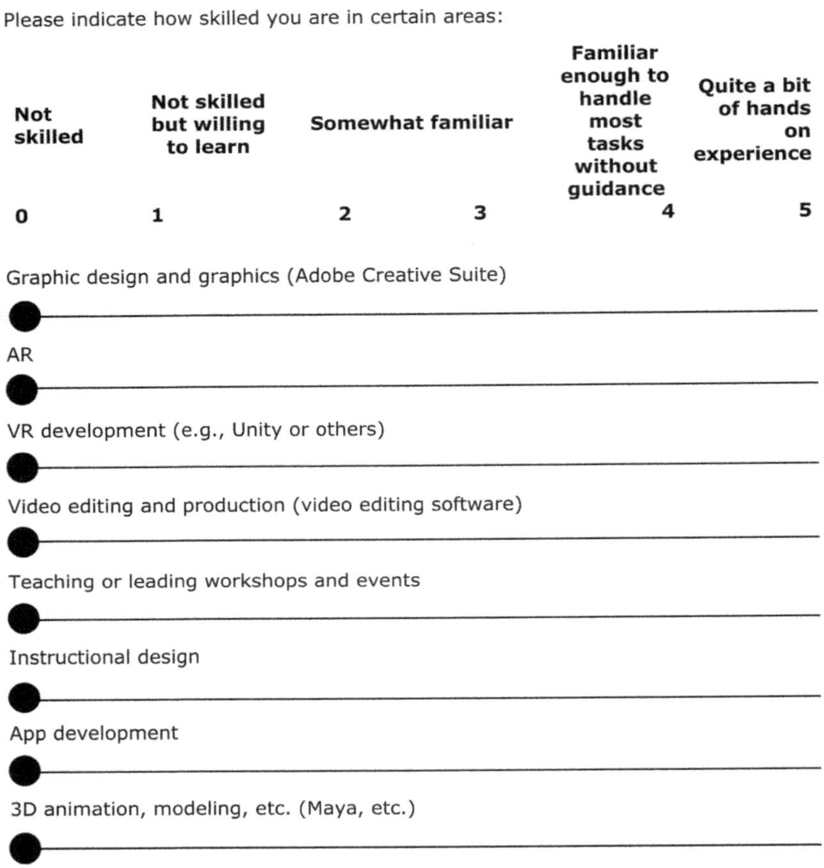

Figure 2-4 Student Skill Survey Questions at a Georgia Tech Research Class

Evaluating Technologies

- What are your desired learning outcomes when using this technology?

  ____

  ____

  ____

  ____

  ____

- What hardware and software do you already have at your institution? (Computers, tablets, OS)
    - Will the VR technology you purchase be compatible with your existing hardware?

- Take an inventory of your existing power and data ports. Review the spec sheets on potential purchases to make sure that the technology you select can connect and communicate with each other through plugs or wirelessly.

- Will the students will be using preexisting content or creating their own content?
    - What digital assets do you have or have access to?
    - What tools do you have for digitizing assets?

- What is the scope of your available time with students to both teach the software and develop the project?

- Are the student skill levels and developmental stages a good match for the technology/project?

- How many students will be working together in the class?

- Will you need someone to approve this project or purchase?

- Who will oversee IT support issues? (See Ch. 3 for more ideas)

Using LEAPS Concepts

The LEAPS concepts can be an initial tool for decision-making for technology solutions. Answer each of these bullet points for your program or organization.

- Learner Analysis
  - Learner preferences
  - Learner professional goals
  - Learner interests
  - Learner preferred modality
- Engagement
  - How much and what interaction level will you have with your students?
  - Face-to-face
  - Online
  - Community involvement
- Accessibility
  - Does the technology support a diverse group of learners?
  - If so, what type? Are there groups of learners that may be excluded if this technology selection is made?
- Purpose of Instruction
  - Align technology solutions with learning objectives, both on a macro and micro level.
- Sustainability
  - How will you maintain this technology over the long term?
  - Cost prohibitive?
  - Is it supported regularly, rapidly changing?

Resources to Follow for Current Ed-Tech Trends

- ALA Trends (https://www.ala.org/tools/future/trends)
- Benchmark (https://www.ala.org/acrl/proftools/benchmark)

- LITA (https://www.ala.org/lita/ttt/)
- Educause (Educause.edu)
- *Wired* magazine (https://www.wired.com/magazine/)
- *Make* magazine (https://makezine.com/tag/makerspaces/)

Evaluating Accessibility Accommodations and Opportunities

- What compliance guidelines does your organization already follow for accessible technology?

  ____

  ____

  ____

  ____

  ____

- What modifications can your VR projects offer?
  - Virtual environment modifications
  - Text-to-speech options
  - Visual settings adjustment options
  - Headset or controller weight

  ____

  ____

  ____

  ____

  ____

- How can your VR Lab space be more welcoming?
  - Adjustable-height tables
  - Screen readers
  - Large monitors
  - Workspaces for left- and right-handed users

- Accessible controls
- Appropriately spaced and navigable room

Evaluating Budget and Financial Needs

- What internal grants does your institution offer?

- What external grants might be available to your program or institution?
  - Federal, state, local, community, or corporate?
  - Consider the timeline for writing, submitting, and enacting the grant, given that you are awarded the funds.

- If you are approaching an administrator, consider your past interactions with them and adjust these tips to best fit your circumstances. Your presentation could identify:
  - how many students this project will reach;
  - the learning outcomes and additional benefits to students through the unique affordances of VR;
  - how your project ties into the school's vision, values, initiatives;
  - how the project will use existing school capital and resources; partnerships with other community resources or corporations;
  - the price per student and how you have considered grants (internal, external) and school-year timing.

____

____

____

____

____

Grant Resources

Major Components of Most Grant Proposals

- Statement of need
- Impact of the research
- Project objectives
- Project description—sample specifics, sampling methods, data collection and security, methodology, tools and technology used or needed, IRB approval
- Evaluation—proposed types of findings and dissemination methods
- Team members, collaborators, contributors, and partnerships—roles, experience, and expertise
- Budget narrative and justification

Open Grants

An increasing number of researchers are sharing their grant proposals openly. They do this to open up research so that all stages of the process can benefit from better interaction and communication and to provide examples for early career researchers writing grants. Ogrants.org

Georgia Tech Office of Sponsored Programs. Most major universities have an office of sponsored programs that can assist you. https://osp.gatech.edu/find-funding

The University of Alabama Proposal Development provides a variety of helpful tools: http://ovpred.ua.edu/office-for-proposal-development/proposal-development/

Gagne's Nine Events of Instruction

Use Gagne's Nine Events of Instruction when designing class activities. Answer the following questions.

1. *How will you gain attention?* In order for learning to occur, you must get the attention of your students.

____

____

____

____

____

2. *Inform learner of the objective.* How will you engage students so that they are aware of the learning objectives and the goals of the educational experience. Reinforce these ideas throughout.

____

____

____

____

____

3. *Stimulate recall of prior information.* What needs to be reinforced?

4. *Present information.* New content should be presented in small digestible chunks to optimize student learning. How might you structure your content into manageable chunks?

5. *What tools and resources will supplement your instruction in order to provide guidance to the students?* What other forms of guidance will you provide? Visuals, tutorials, partnerships with other professionals, demonstrations?

6. *How will you integrate milestones in order to elicit performance?* Practice activities, status reports? Students will need to demonstrate periodically that they are learning the material being presented or the information they are studying.

7. *Provide feedback at critical milestone points.* What kinds of feedback would be useful to the students based on the activities you are designing and the milestones you created?

8. *Assess performance.* How will overall performance be evaluated? Share rubrics and your evaluation methods with students, and in some cases cocreate rubrics with the students.

9. *Enhance retention and transfer of information.* How might students apply what they have learned through their project activities? How might they use these skills outside the classroom? Repetition of learning activities can reinforce concepts in the classroom, increasing the chances students will utilize the skill set beyond the classroom environment. Perhaps ask students to reflect on this before leaving the project or class.

THREE

Technology Design and Decisions: Refine Your Technology Solutions

Two of the key drivers behind program development and resource acquisition will be the strategic goals of the organization and its existing technology infrastructure. It is advisable to look over your organization's strategic plan in detail and connect the goals of your service to the overarching goals of your institution or school. As mentioned in previous sections, after outlining a mission statement for your program, your service or project managers will want to perform a SWOT analysis. A SWOT analysis is a strategic planning technique that helps your team analyze internal Strengths and Weaknesses, along with external Opportunities and Threats. Using this analysis will help you identify existing strengths in your organization or program. Additionally, it helps your team recognize where there is opportunity for growth or collaboration, as well as identifying challenges that could prevent you from reaching your long-term goals. With these elements in mind, you will want to assess your current technology infrastructure and determine if this hardware and software can meet the goals of your program.

See the strategic planning SWOT questions in the resources at the end of the chapter to guide your initial evaluations.

Any program that engages students with emerging technologies such as AR, VR, or MR should begin with looking at what devices your organization already offers access to, and what devices you still need to acquire as they align with your program goals.

BACKGROUND: DEVICE COLLECTION AND SPACE

Device Collection Development

Similar to a specialized collection of books or scholarly resources for a particular subject area, an emerging technologies program or class is supported by a device collection. Thus, when designing a new AR/VR program, one of the most important decisions service managers need to make is centered around building out the device collection. Devices, to some extent, determine the scope of potential projects, the technical skills required, and the learning curve expected. Therefore, it is critical to have a clear service vision to guide device acquisition. For instance, a college-level collection is likely to support larger-scale projects, while most K–12 school collections may be focused on smaller projects. At Georgia Tech, the service vision is focused on giving students access to several device types representing varying levels of technical sophistication. This robust collection encourages diverse project designs and fosters educational curiosity. In general, the library strives to improve access to advanced technologies for community members regardless of background or discipline. K–12 schools could also have ambitious research initiatives, sometimes even in partnership with other research institutions or local organizations. Mount Vernon's upper school students worked with Children's Healthcare of Atlanta to create a VR program for patients going through physical therapy (Mount Vernon School 2020). When classes are designed around these technologies, it is also critical to keep in mind that class projects done for academic credits are likely to be more demanding than casual projects done as an extracurricular activity. In general, your community interests and potential scope of work drive the device collection development.

As AR/VR/MR devices have been improving technologically and increasing in number in the past several years, there is a spectrum of devices to choose from. On the expensive side, the high-end devices have gone through multiple iterations to improve the user experience. Newer devices are addressing challenges such as motion sickness. They are also lowering the weight of these devices, and gradually moving toward untethering from the computer. At the same time, there are more affordable options available on the market. Combining the budget constraints and user needs will help narrow down the selection of devices.

Wikipedia provides detailed comparisons of available VR (2022) and MR (2022) headsets based on cost, features, ease of use/setup, software requirements, capacity of the device, integration with other tools, and frequency of updates (https://en.wikipedia.org/wiki/Comparison_of_virtual_reality_headsets). As always, remember that Wikipedia is a living document maintained by the community, so use the comparison chart as a guide to start your own research and verification of specs.

Building a Device Collection at a Higher-Ed School

Over the years of managing, upgrading and utilizing the devices, the Georgia Tech library developed three guidelines for device purchases:

1. *Diversity.* The collection should provide users with options consisting of both more advanced and easy-to-use devices. The higher-end products usually are more complicated to learn but also give users a lot more control over the design. On the other hand, the lower-end products are easier to use but less flexible or customizable. As of spring 2022, most of the advanced devices are still tethered to a PC that uses a powerful graphics card.
2. *Compatibility.* At each price range of devices, purchase decisions should be made considering the compatibility between the devices and the accompanying computer workstations, if applicable. This prevents the service (VR lab, institution) from falling into the trap of needing extra hardware to drive the devices, which could increase organizational expenses beyond the threshold of the device costs.
3. *Sustainability.* Beyond the initial device acquisition, Georgia Tech Library service managers also consider providing sustainable access to the devices. For example, if one of the devices breaks, the lab needs to have a backup in place to keep the service available. If not, the service/lab needs to purchase a new one or have a quick repair channel available for rapid turnaround. In this case, service contracts with institutionally supported vendors can be one avenue to support such devices. In the long term, any program that relies heavily on emerging technologies needs a plan in place to retire old devices and update the collection every few years. Following the retirement of older devices, new purchases need to provide a consistent and comparable level of

technological capacities. To keep this device collection development sustainable, these considerations need to be codified in the service plan when designing your program and should be reflected in the service budget proposals. A tangential budget consideration is identifying if your selected program requires individual seat licenses for each user. As you are selecting your devices, identify whether software requires a one-time fee or a recurring subscription fee.

The device acquisition process begins with budget approval. Based on available devices, selections are made with all criteria considered to create an affordable, accessible, and sustainable collection.

Building Device Collection at a K–12 School

For schools with limited resources, an avenue to maintaining a diverse and sustainable device collection is to consider corporate partnerships. These connections benefit both institutions, drive research efforts, and allow beta testing of new technologies. Sometimes the connections between educational institutions and enterprises may already exist. Other times your institution may reach out to corporations, such as Mount Vernon building a partnership with Dell/Alienware (Mount Vernon School 2018).

Mount Vernon instructors researched the VR industry and connected with VR experts through social media and LinkedIn to share their teaching interests and device needs. Through nurturing a partnership with the Dell/Alienware Corporation, Dell/Alienware sent the school VR equipment for students to use. With these devices students conduct "real-time VR research" in the collaborative Virtual Reality Lab at the school. The content that students created relates to a variety of industries, including the Center for Civil and Human Rights in Atlanta and the Children's Hospital of Atlanta (Toller 2018).

Space for Immersive Technology

Technology solutions are a combination of both strategic vision and realistic measures given the constraints of an organization's infrastructure. In most cases, schools or institutions do not have the luxury of building out a physical lab or service from scratch. Even in cases where most of the service is new, there is some dependency on a legacy infrastructure. For instance, designers may be limited by the location of certain data ports or power supplies even in a completely new space. Envisioning probable-use cases and class projects will assist your team in prioritizing space features, optimizing space design, and maximizing the available technologies and resources. Educators will need to evaluate the supporting hardware and software, along with the physical footprint and infrastructure required to meet educational needs.

Currently, there are two approaches for space design. Either the organization could subscribe to one of the all-in-one packages, or the service managers would design a space based on the devices they have and their current technology infrastructure.

There are businesses offering hardware, software, and training all-in-one classroom VR programs for educators. These programs save time setting up needed resources but may lack the flexibility to accommodate a custom device collection. Some require a recurring subscription fee, as well. Other companies, as of 2022, include ClassVR (https://www.classvr.com/), SMALLab (https://www.smallablearning.com/), and zSpace (https://zspace.com/). Each company offers a slightly different range of devices, interactivity, and educational content. For example, ClassVR offers individual headsets that connect wirelessly to a central headset management portal where educators can "view and monitor student progress" through "state-aligned curriculum" (classvr.com). ClassVR also promotes their bright orange portable, "secure storage and charging" cases to hold the headsets (ClassVR, n.d.). The SMALLab technology engages the entire classroom as a "3D mixed reality learning environment" that uses a motion capture system and overhead projector to create a physically interactive learning space for students (https://www.smallablearning.com/smallab). Like ClassVR, the SMALLab subscription also offers "standards-aligned activities" that educators can choose from (SMALLab). The zSpace Inspire also does not use a "head-mounted display," but instead uses a laptop-like machine with integrated motion tracking and stylus for interacting with 3D programs (zSpace, n.d.).

As ideal as the all-in-one packages sound, most educational organizations are choosing to customize the immersive technology space themselves, especially at the beginning of their programming. One reason for this, other than overall flexibility, is cost. With a limited budget to work with, service managers are careful to select technology and only fund equipment and materials where it is needed the most. Also, institutions tend to pilot a small-scale service using as many existing resources as possible before scaling up.

Virtual Reality Space at a Higher-Ed School

A powerful workstation is needed in order to use some XR devices and to develop some projects. For instance, students from the research section class usually use Unity in developing their class projects, which must run on a workstation. Not to mention if students choose one of the tethered devices for their projects, they have no choice but to reserve a workstation with advanced graphic cards to drive the project rendering. This use case requires the library to have a dedicated workspace with computers for AR/VR/XR content development.

The Georgia Tech Library has gone through numerous phases to locate an appropriate service area for AR/VR devices. When this team started in 2018, there were two tethered devices, one HTC Vive, one Oculus Rift. They were set up on two workstations in the Data Visualization lab pilot space. These workstations had high usage data, which prompted the library to consider an independent service and a new space dedicated solely to AR/VR. At the same time, the library was going through the LibraryNEXT initiative, which included a complete building renovation. The AR/VR service went through the project management review process to establish itself as a separate service temporarily located in an open space on the second floor Innovation and Ideation service area. AR/VR went dormant during the COVID pandemic due to remote work and device sanitation concerns. In the summer of 2022, the librarians and IT professionals got together to review the location for AR/VR research and determined that it would fit into the technology-themed third floor to colocate with High Performance Computing, Data Visualization, and the Media Scholarship Commons. Before the completion of this more permanently structured space reconfiguration, the service was temporarily located on the first floor of the library across from the main entrance to the building. This space was chosen in order to maintain a designated service location and increase visibility for the library visitors.

A VR Lab at a K–12 School

The instructors at Mount Vernon identified a few key qualities in their space as they developed the program. One feature they found helpful is a centralized workstation in the lab where they could organize the class and demonstrate content. This workstation provides instructors with a functional space to share information with the entire class before the group splits to work individually or in small groups at local computer stations. The capacity of sharing content with the whole class not only saves time that would be otherwise used to explain the same content to individuals repeatedly, but also switches the class pace between group work and class discussion to help students focus. Another key to the success of the space is to keep it flexible, especially when circumstances or room layouts change. For instance, when the Mount Vernon VR Lab moved to a new building location, their new space had too many windows, and the amount of natural light coming in overwhelmed the display of the HTC Vive headset. The instructors had to reorient the VR Lab layout to more effectively use the HTC headset.

Student-Centric Learning

Having completed a thorough needs assessment and analysis of equipment including headsets, technology infrastructure, and space requirements, librarians must focus on what resources are needed for content creation. Instructors and librarians must facilitate gathering information from students about how the students envision using these emerging technologies. Student aspirations can help drive this discussion.

Central to this understanding is:

1. What are the students' interests and technical proficiency as they relate to the local curriculum?
2. What are the available resources for the students?

In a classroom setting, the project design is a collaborative process between instructors and students. Instructors gather information from students about the project ideas that they are passionate about, and how they envision using these technologies to implement the project ideas. The process is iterative, where the students present their plans, then the instructors help refine the design based on the technical feasibility and proposed workload. The designs may be streamlined or augmented depending on the feasibility assessment (student skill level, available technology, time constraints). For a semester-long course (fifteen to seventeen weeks) involving VR design, such as the case study from Georgia Tech, project teams should have their initial design ready for implementation on the VR devices four weeks into the semester to allow ample time for testing and implementation. The goal is to encourage students in experimentation and hands-on learning. This student-centric learning style creates a collaborative and individualized learning environment addressing students' "varying levels of ability and different interests." It also allows students to learn and proceed at their own pace (Richmond 2017). For a class environment, instructors can use student proposals as a tool for documenting and guiding the project implementation. Proposals can serve as a structured mechanism for capturing initial student design ideas. By creating a structured proposal, instructors can assist the students in focusing on certain key components and keeping the project scope manageable. Additionally, building in time for design modifications based on instructor feedback will be critical as the project moves forward. For nonclassroom settings, focus groups or user surveys can assist program managers in tailoring a service for user or customer needs.

After the initial design is in place, akin to the role of a project manager, instructors can scan the local environment for potential resources students can use for their implementation. These resources can be materials incorporated into the design, like archival materials, audio/video content, free game assets, free sound effects, and so on. Resources can also be tools the students need to complete their projects but are not readily available, such as specialized cameras, 3D scanners, specialized software, and support. These resources can sometimes be found within other departments of your own organization. Other times, it means outreach to neighboring organizations in the same area, such as a local makerspace. Partnerships can be a valuable part of developing new programs.

For institutions creating classes or programming with emerging technologies as a core component, we suggest integrating troubleshooting, solution research, and peer review as part of the curriculum. Your students will become partners with you in solving issues related to hardware, software, coding, and testing. Consider developing your curriculum around workflow problem-solving experiences. This will give students real-world troubleshooting experience.

See Figures 2-2 and 2-3 in Chapter 2 resources for a student-technology matching questionnaire.

One key to this learning process is to be flexible in order to accommodate the project timelines and budgetary issues along the way. Most changes come from technical challenges with the headset device or coding. Sometimes the IT support team may not be able to deliver the desired solution immediately; other times, students can be stuck at certain code errors. Both situations can cause delays to this work. Therefore, planning time for unexpected changes, or a project design change to address especially hard issues, are critical for completing the project on time. The design process will be explained in more detail in Chapter 4.

DESIGNING TECHNOLOGY SOLUTIONS

As noted earlier, the first step toward designing technological solutions is building the collection of devices, whether through purchases or partnerships. With the device selection settled, library service managers then move to evaluate the supporting hardware and software for VR initiatives, along with the physical footprint and infrastructure required to meet the educational needs. Further consideration must be given to how this technology and the space are supported.

On-Demand IT Support

For projects or initiatives that include a certain level of dependency on reliable technology, students face both expected and unexpected challenges. For this reason, anticipating project timeline adjustments is an essential part of designing technology solutions. At the same time, identifying information technology (IT) partners and coming to an understanding on support expectations prior to launching a service or designing a class should be part of the technical design decisions.

Therefore, part of the IT support design process should involve service management plans and developing strategies for collaboration with IT professionals. Leveraging their expertise will become crucial once a project is under way. Educators who enlist the help of colleagues outside of their immediate department may want to explore the possibility of a memo of understanding (MOU) or a service expectation contract to ensure technical assistance will be there for the students. These types of discussions remove the possibility of any kind of miscommunication regarding the support your program or class needs.

Some frequent support needs that should be considered and planned around include:

- Hardware updates
- Device purchases, maintenance, and upgrades
- Software purchase and licensing

- Account management
- Software troubleshooting
- Content storage and transfer

On the hardware side, most device controllers need charging or a battery to work; some older versions of devices had irregular connection issues. When students have critical deadlines to meet and multiple priorities, if any issues arise in the middle of the semester or during class, it requires immediate attention. Instructors are often the point of contact for resolving these issues. If the instructors cannot troubleshoot these issues themselves, having a network of technology specialists available is advisable. Instructors need to consider flexible approaches to their lesson plan as these technical challenges cannot always be predicted. For example, allowing students to submit documentation or a change request explaining how their project timeline is being modified due to unexpected challenges teaches both communication skills and project management concepts. Other issues can be better predicted and planned for, such as scheduled device updates.

On the software side, programs need accurate account log-ins and frequent software updates. When users need to download specific apps for testing, it is possible they will need IT support as the download function could be locked down to administrative privileges. The security protocol for publicly available workstations is another important consideration that can, in some cases, require IT staff assistance. The most popular AR/VR/MR development tool, Unity, is a cross-platform game engine developed by Unity Technologies. A common challenge for students working with Unity is managing issues related to frequent and irregular updates to the software. (See examples of the update releases here: https://unity3d.com/get-unity/download/archive.) In the labs at the K–12 and higher education levels, failure to install these updates immediately could cause the project code to not run, and therefore, an immediate stop of the research.

Another main challenge relating to programming that involves specialized software is account management for devices and public workstations. Oculus headsets require log-in to pair the controllers and headsets. Oculus and the Microsoft Store require a log-in account to download apps and games. Some other VR resources also require accounts to sign in and use the equipment or assets. Different organizations have varying levels of computer security on public stations in a lab or any shared resources for the students. Cybersecurity can be very institute specific depending on the local network and the type of activities the organization engages in. For security and safety reasons, institutions usually have designated accounts for these resources to avoid inadvertently exposing personal or research information. Managing accounts can also help institutions with content control and maintain student focus on the specific educational goals at hand. Just as they curate collections of books and other traditional resources, librarians and educators in this area should curate the digital content for the specific learning outcomes associated with the AR/VR programs and the goals of the organization. However, effectively and securely managing accounts and sharing them with incoming users pose a challenge to the technology-related work. For instance, as of 2022, Oculus and STEAM stores require one-point or single-user accounts, rather than educational licenses or an institutional account. This one-point requirement often means that students must use personal accounts or otherwise less-regulated access points, if allowed at all in their schools. Depending on the program, IT requirements, and licenses, the service managers will need to determine if each individual user has a separate log-in or if the log-ins are shared and saved under a class or institutional account.

IT Support at a Higher-Ed School

At Georgia Tech, librarians closely collaborate with IT professionals on device purchases, maintenance, and upgrades to guarantee a project development process with minimum interruptions due to technical issues.

The wide range of technical issues the team encountered posed a steep learning curve for the IT professionals and librarians alike. IT and the librarians had to work closely to track usage patterns, monitor help requests, and provide students with a quick communication channel for assistance. During the first few semesters of the research class, an on-demand IT support model was needed to address unexpected interruptions in the student workflow. An ad hoc on-demand model for VR technology help requests was developed in response to some of these challenges. Under this model, within specified time periods, such as during designated student research hours, the library IT team would give primary attention to VR support requests. VR help requests were triaged and assigned a priority level. If the request involved a critical failure in the technology causing a stoppage in all work, IT support would meet with students within minutes of the request. Lower-level priority issues were addressed usually within the week after IT support could research the problem further. This tiered support structure was beneficial in that it prevented major interruption of the teaching or research. Therefore, when developing a class or research project that involves the heavy use of emerging technologies, designing a tiered support framework in collaboration with your IT partners will ensure a seamless educational experience.

A positive by-product of collecting the data about past help requests was that it informed the future students' learning experience. Over time, the request data offers insight on repeating and predictable issues that IT can proactively check and schedule maintenance over. Essentially, the support structure created a knowledge base for librarians and IT staff.

The library also collaborated with IT professionals to create a specialized account for STEAM and Oculus game stores so only educational games were purchased and downloaded for students to play.

IT Support at a K–12 School

Among various IT support issues, account management is of particular importance for K–12 schools as we are working with minors (students under the age of eighteen) or primary school students (as some programs do not allow users under the age of thirteen). The instructors at Galloway found that some programs were easier to work with than others in a 9–12 high school computer lab environment. These programs often offer individual educational licenses for each "seat" or user, or a single institutional account that the instructor could centrally control. Instructors can use the central account to set the types of access the students have to various features, stores, and content areas of each program. Some of these programs were Unity, Unreal, Adobe, and HTC Vive.

The account situation for Oculus and STEAM stores poses extra challenge to K–12 students. With limited IT support, students may log in as themselves, which exposes their personal information to access and vulnerability on a public/shared computer. Additionally, since the instructor is not able to limit the store/community resources to educational only, the students may be able to purchase inappropriate items or access nonacademic content. If your class must use these systems, it is important to educate them on responsible and safe digital behaviors so that these concerns and behavioral expectations are top-of-mind while students are working in the programs.

Additional Considerations

An additional consideration when assessing the technology design is the logistics behind data storage for resource-intensive work such as AR/VR. As you plan for where the students will be doing the bulk of their research or work, there need to be storage options available for them. If students are working on library workstations, they will need a way to save and back up work created on shared workspaces. Files associated with this type of work can be large or dependent on other data files. For example, with certain applications, work in progress is automatically saved to hard drive locations where the software is installed. One example is iMovie; this software automatically saves as the user edits their work, but in doing so iMovie saves unrendered projects to the application folder on the computer. Unfinished work can be later exported as a library, but this process is not intuitive to the general user. Researching appropriate cloud storage solutions or shared network locations for large files should be included in the planning process.

The challenges and considerations listed should all be analyzed when starting a program that incorporates AR/VR/MR so that policies, procedures and support resources are outlined early in the planning process. Being aware of the challenges will allow for the smooth implementation of technological solutions. For institutions without extensive IT resources or a substantial technology budget, much of the IT support will fall to the instructors or program managers themselves. In this case, it is important during the external environmental scan to consult with other institutions that are already offering this kind of educational programming. Additionally, there may be opportunities to partner with other units in your organization or student groups in order to create a support framework. Creating a knowledge base of IT issues, frequently asked questions, and technology solutions ahead of time will help an organization plan out support and maintenance moving forward.

However, it is unlikely that service managers will come up with seamless plans. It is more realistic to have a tentative plan in place at the beginning of any programming. As time goes by, more institution-specific use cases will emerge. These use cases should be documented, and appropriate configurations and technology decisions should be integrated into the original design. As noted

See Chapter 5 for more information about community building and the resources at the end of Chapter 5 for starter questions to ask peer institutions about their programs.

previously, working with emerging technologies is always an iterative process to accommodate the rapidly changing environment. Staying flexible and collaborating with specialists can be critical to the success (or failure) of your curriculum and meeting the learning objectives.

Security and Responsible User Behavior

Computer networks and the internet are becoming increasingly important in education; this is especially true for a technology-driven learning process like AR/VR/MR development. This reliance on networked resources potentially exposes devices to attacks of viruses and malware. Different organizations have different levels of device and software security. Any organization wishing to provide students with the hardware and software to support their AR/VR projects will want to assess how best to integrate an organization's cybersecurity measures with user policies.

When mapping out the IT support plan, one key challenge is to balance ease of access with security. Organizations must balance network security versus ease of access for the students utilizing shared resources for secure and sustainable use of these technologies. For instance, administrative permissions and network blocks can lower the cyber risks, but they also present hurdles to the students who are working on software that requires frequent updates, installations, plug-ins, or modifications as part of the development workflow. As such, the library IT support team must account for this when providing students access to publicly available workstations and in setting up user privileges relating to their development work. Service managers should plan for a support framework that takes network security, account management, and storage solutions into account. Some solutions to consider include creating special log-in profiles, separate computer images or subnets, and specific access privileges for students working with emerging technologies. To effectively manage network security while meeting students' needs will require working closely with IT partners to design and develop flexible user policies and system modification permissions.

It's important to keep in mind that no active system can be impervious to hacks or attacks. Sensible security approaches are techniques to "mitigate risk" and reduce the probability and extent of a cyberattack (Pichman 2019). When designing a security plan, it's also important to consider how your students/users will actually engage with the technology. If participants circumvent security measures or act against policy because they do not understand the purpose/gravity, then the security measure is not very effective.

Education resources of responsible digital behavior are available through different organizations. Digital citizenship standards for students can be found through the Providence Day School's Digital Compass and the International Society for Technology in Education's Student Standards section 1.2 (ISTE 2016; Providence Day School, n.d.). Standards listed through these sources emphasize six to seven valuable skills. Briefly, students ought to cultivate their digital presence and reputation just as they would in real life. They should understand "nothing is private" and learn ways to manage digital privacy, security, data collection, and their own personal data (Providence Day School, n.d.).

Students benefit from understanding the permanence of their digital actions. Digital citizenship skills worded positively as "do's" give learners strategies to strive for, rather than a long list of "don'ts" to avoid (see examples at https://digcitcommit.org/). Some of these digital citizenship skills help students learn how to respect and give credit to others when using or sharing content. Some programs also include students learning about perspective and bias evaluation when consuming digital content, just as they would for other print or audio media. These programs also suggest students refresh their digital manners, learning how to act in "positive, safe, legal, and ethical behavior" in the digital realm (ISTE 2016). Reviewing these skills is especially important for K–12 programs as students may not yet have established these technology norms. Of course, even with older students, it is important to make sure everyone is on the same page for behavior expectations from the start.

At the beginning of classes or programs, while the class is testing log-ins and installing updates, consider adding a "Best Practices Unit" to review digital citizenship skills. This unit can include content about general technological practices and skills, including when or how to share personal information, presenting oneself online, making usernames/passwords, file management and backing up resources, regularly saving work, downloading securely, and so on. Finally, most digital citizenship skills emphasize how students must learn to balance their use of digital technology and their engagement in the "real world," including managing distractions, which can be a difficult skill for users of all ages to master! In all cases, we recommend not taking the students' knowledge for granted. Emphasizing, practicing, and reviewing responsible digital behavior goes a long way.

Logistical Considerations: Access to Headsets and Other Technologies

Easy and seamless access to the devices and physical space is one of the key pillars to support educational programming that includes the use of emerging technologies on the XR spectrum. In contrast to the technologies traditionally hosted in libraries, such as computers, printers, and keyboards, XR devices, (primarily VR and MR) are smaller in size. Some XR devices can be tethered and some untethered from a computer workstation, and therefore need to be managed separately to avoid issues such as device loss, damage, or a missing battery. These devices fall into the category of computer peripherals when it comes to managing them. Service managers and instructors need to think about the logistics of making the devices and supporting equipment easily available to students without substantial inventory loss or damage.

VR headsets or device lending programs can serve a dual purpose. In a general sense, library hardware lending programs can provide students who might not otherwise have access to these devices the opportunity to experiment with new technologies at minimal to no cost for both academic and personal use (DeCristofaro, Hutter, and Tanzi 2020). Additionally, if an academic or school library can integrate the lending program alongside its curriculum, this could be a built-in way to track student usage of the devices and ensure equal access and equal time with the technologies. Depending on how class assignments are structured (group work or individual assignments), students will likely need to rotate these devices with the other members of their class. A library lending program can create device and headset policies for this use case. This might be best accomplished through a subset of the collection being set aside for course assignment use. The program can either reserve dedicated devices to be checked out by class instructors and students during the semester or, alternatively, if the devices are limited, class-use-only policy could be set up for specific time ranges throughout the day or week.

Managing Logistics at a Higher-Ed School

The logistics of managing a dedicated VR service in a library can be challenging. For the limited number of VR devices, students are likely to find themselves competing with library users from other classes or departments not only on access to these resources, but also in finding available space and support for using the resources. Students may also physically share this technology with other institutions or community spaces depending on the availability of device models in the collection. A library device lending program in place with the ability to triage requests or add levels of priority to the collection could be a way to address the issue of limited availability and high demand. Additionally, setting aside a collection of devices or equipment for in-lab use only will ensure students are able to physically access the equipment while in the library. Although it does not address the needs of students requiring the ability to work off campus, outside the library, or at home, this solution can provide some measure of access for students who need to work on-site. At Georgia Tech, the device lending program is integrated into the discovery system and catalog for checkout (see Figure 3-1). The hardware and peripheries in this collection have specific loan periods and forms that users sign to ensure equipment is returned in good working condition (Georgia Tech Library, n.d.b). Outside of these reserved devices or specified time windows, access to the devices would be open to the rest of the community to balance designated use and general accessibility. The general idea is that the library should consider not only individual use of technical resources, but how an organization addresses coordinated use of devices between groups or classes of students when these users are trying to meet assignment deadlines under certain time constraints.

Another logistical consideration is space management. The available space for VR use and development needs to be reservable, just like the devices. Additionally, the window of time for the reservation of the devices and the space should align. For instance, if a device can be checked out for four hours, so should the room or designated space. This is a seemingly intuitive model; however, it is not easily accomplishable. One of the challenges is that for most libraries or organizations, there is no system in place for the peripherals checkout system to speak to the room reservation system. This causes users to not only have to reserve them as two separate processes, but also potential misalignment between the reservable time windows of the two. Having space reservation systems and device lending systems that can communicate with each other and align is an important consideration for these types of technologies and a current challenge.

At Georgia Tech, students need to reserve the VR device and room separately. The headsets and accompanying devices can be checked out for four hours due to an approximate estimate of the time needed for a project session, while the room reservation system only allows two hours per reservation. To avoid this reservation misalignment and system issue, students must make an additional two-hour reservation once their room reservation starts. This is, however, not guaranteed if someone else already reserved the next two hours at an earlier time. Having compatible systems that can effectively communicate with each other or consolidating these two facets of the service would be a major user experience improvement and significantly simplify the workflow.

Managing Logistics at a K–12 School

At Mount Vernon, students are welcome to use the VR Lab during classes and during specific club meeting times. Unlike the Georgia Tech model, students at Mount Vernon are not allowed to check out VR devices or reserve the lab space individually. The VR club can coordinate with their club sponsor, a school faculty member, if the students need additional time to work on projects. Since students can only work with the VR devices in person with faculty members present, this approach allows the instructor to provide direct troubleshooting support to students. The in-person interaction allows the instructor to keep an eye on the functionality of the hardware and ensure systems are working properly. Outside of the classroom and class meeting time, students work on other aspects of the project that do not interface directly with the VR hardware. Students might do design work related to their project or work on software to create 3D models. They might also research how VR is being used in the professional world of medicine or architecture or explore the idea of artists using VR in their creations.

Reservation Systems

Trouble-free availability of the devices and access to space are crucial to the success of the service. If a library finds they have a small or limited collection of headsets and similar devices, organizational or local collaboration on device sharing offers a possible solution. Along with the devices is the space in which they are used. An easy-to-use room reservation system comes into play here. The reservation system with the best user experience is one that is easy to check and request for users and easy to maintain for library staff, such as the popular library reservation tool SpringShare's LibCal, if funding is available. See an image of the Georgia Tech Gadgets Reservation page, which uses SpringShare, in Figure 3-1 (Georgia Tech Library. n.d.a). Finally, a user-friendly backup system and storage tool helps students store, transfer, and share their ongoing projects with their teammates. Some basic experience with these tools, such as GitHub, early in the class helps

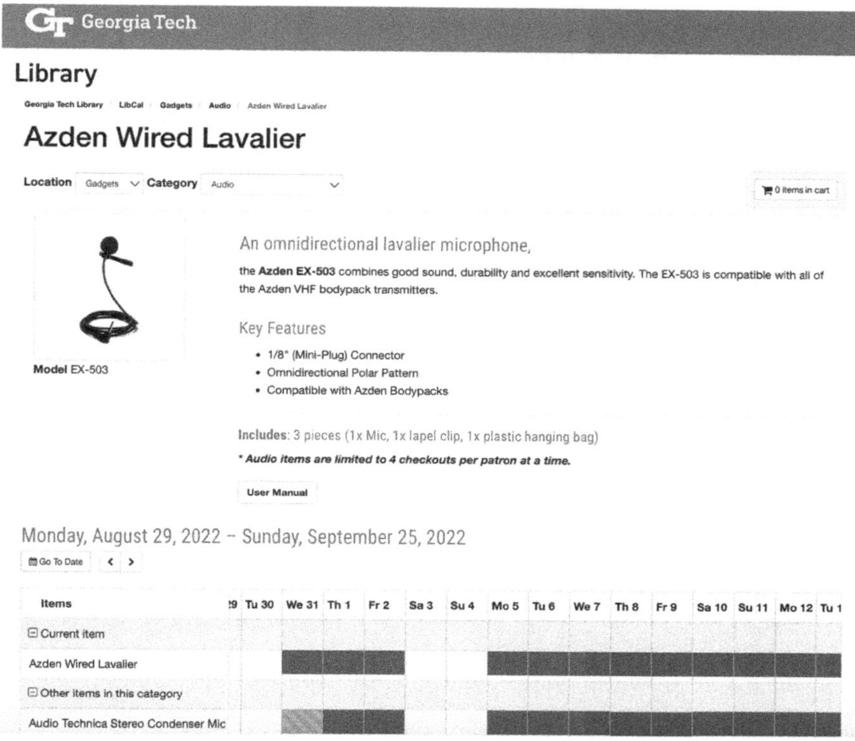

Figure 3-1 Georgia Tech Library Gadget Reservation page for Azden wired lavalier with reservation calendar

alleviate student concerns about losing project artifacts later in the process. With many factors to consider in project development, students should start the class with a plan of managing, documenting, saving, and sharing their work with the team as well as instructors to guarantee updated, transparent communication and timely support for the issues they may encounter.

Time Management

When it comes to a class involving AR/VR development, time management is one factor contributing to learner success. Available time is a factor that will influence the type of projects your students can accomplish and the level of technological complexity you can incorporate into student research. As noted by Nguyen et al. in their research study from 2019, the software and hardware learning curves in AR/VR research, as well as the time involved in learning a new programming language, were one of the biggest constraints as expressed by their students. It takes time to learn languages such as C# and get familiar with the Integrated Development Environments (IDEs). Putting these skills into practice is especially time-consuming (Nguyen, Jung, and Dang 2019). Additionally, this study noted that the most time-consuming part of the student work was the creation of 3D models. As a result, 25 percent of the students in their observations decided to download and reuse existing models. This was something that the team at Georgia Tech noted with our students as well. In the Georgia Tech research classes, students were encouraged to find reusable assets to practice with, when possible, especially for beginners. Once students master working with existing models, only then would we encourage designing original 3D models from basic shapes. Allowing students to use pre-created models lets them shift focus from the intricacies of 3D modeling to creating scripts for interactions, which is widely considered one of the more challenging tasks and at the core of project implementation (Nguyen, Jung, and Dang 2019). One alternative solution that instructors can utilize to create a framework that promotes effective use of time is having the class or team split into functional roles. For instance, this could involve having one part of the class or a subset of students work solely on designing models, while other students focus on different areas of the project, such as debugging or coding in Unity.

Tasks like creating 3D models can easily consume a few weeks of time over the course of the semester and leave students less time than needed to finish other tasks necessary for the completion of their project. To navigate through the project design, students at Georgia Tech are encouraged to use pre-created assets as much as possible to simplify each step of the workflow. After the basic structure is in place, students are then encouraged to explore ways of polishing their projects like creating their own 3D models or developing other customized components.

Breaking the class up into sub-teams can be an effective way to prepare students for the same dynamics of collaboration one might find in the professional world beyond the college experience. The final model of collaboration on teams depends on students' research interests and skill sets, as discussed in the earlier chapters.

Find resources on locating reusable 3D models in the chapter resources.

Time is also a consideration with respect to equal allocation of resources. If your program has more students than VR devices, consider if students will share the devices as they work individually or while working in teams. As mentioned before, some institutions set up a reservation system where students can schedule their visit to the computer lab or check out materials during a certain time in order to distribute access fairly and in a structured manner. Consider how much of the workload will depend on directly interacting with the devices (hardware, software, coding, user-testing, etc.) and how much can be accomplished through more flexible uses (design theory, game planning, etc.).

Time is a key factor of project design. Identify whether your students have an entire school year, a semester, a quarter, a few weeks, or a long weekend to work on this project. Each of these intervals will determine what type of project is possible.

Some sample projects for each of these time frames can be found in the resources at the end of the chapter.

After considering the overall time available to you and your students (semester, a few weeks, etc.), instructors leading projects that emphasize the use of technology will want to evaluate time requirements for:

1. *The Essentials and Basic Requirements.* A starting point is foundational technical skills. This could include orienting students on how to access hardware, software, headset devices, and needed resources. Other considerations are calculating the time for installing software, updating credentials, and making sure students can log in or access compatible programs. Additionally, this may be the stage of the project to assign simple instant-gratification learning exercises, or a quick win to motivate the students in moving forward. Technology-rich projects can be challenging, and it will be important to integrate positive reinforcement throughout your curriculum. Consider including a basic exercise such as successfully logging in and creating a new file or project with no content, as an early graded assignment.

2. *Self-Learning.* Once students have familiarized themselves with how to access the needed hardware and software, allow them time to self-explore. The amount of time an instructor allocates for self-learning can vary based on the complexity of the overall project. Self-learning will inform project development. Making a clear distinction between the basic logistics of accessing resources and most of their other learning activities will allow students the bandwidth to absorb new skills necessary for development within platforms such as Unity. Having already mastered the basics of logging in and accessing resources allows students to focus solely

on curated tutorials and articles as assigned by the instructor. During this phase, it may be important to assign students readings or case studies that spotlight specific use cases that involve the use of AR/VR. Beginning students may need practical examples of how these technologies are being used in industry to inspire their project ideas.

3. *Project Ideation and Development.* A project is only as good as a well-conceived plan. Depending on the complexity of the curriculum and the overall time-frame parameters, time should be allocated for project proposals and an implementation plan. Being able to assess the feasibility of student ideas earlier in the process saves time and eliminates the need for excessive trial and error in development and implementation. In some cases, instructors may be conceptualizing and assigning learning activities or project ideas, thus taking on more responsibility for this component of the work. In other situations, students may build on what they have learned in earlier parts of the class and propose a project for consideration independently. In either case, a scaffolded learning approach is ideal where students progressively build knowledge and skills in distinct phases culminating in the realization of the project concept.

4. *Scaffolding.* Regardless of the scope of the project, a scaffolded approach can be beneficial, and your time requirements can be organized based on that framework. Beginning with a simple orientation of needed resources, sample exercises, and finally building up to a larger-scale project allows students to approach their work in manageable chunks. A beginning sample exercise to orient students to a virtual environment might be asking them to integrate 360 photos in virtual reality mode using Google Cardboard with a smartphone or tablet. This scaffolded approach also allows students to self-organize into working groups and benefit from peer learning.

5. *Reflection, Critique, Peer Learning.* Building in time for critiques and peer feedback before the conclusion of the project will allow students to learn from one another. Prior to final projects being submitted, allow the students to first reflect on their own work and then other students' work. Components to these reflective documents can be technologies used, challenges encountered, statement of purpose, and lessons learned. Encouraging transparency and cooperation between students will give them another avenue for learning. This also gives them the opportunity to correct course before submitting their final work. Taking feedback from both instructors and fellow students and

See the resources at the end of the chapter for sample reflection questions from a Georgia Tech research class.

building in the time for them to adjust their projects based on that feedback integrate the critical idea of user experience into their work.

Additional situations to consider when planning the curriculum that could have an impact on a project timeline:

- Maintaining backups for any equipment and asset documentation (including hardware/software serial numbers)
- Verifying compatibility between hardware and software
- Documenting program crashes and causes
- Wi-Fi stability or direct Ethernet connection
- Safeguard against lost files—redundancy or backups
- Manage stolen or broken items and their replacement process
- Planning for device or hardware repairs and turnaround times

Throughout this reading, we emphasize that an activity you may consider prior to any work beginning is a skills survey to determine each student's level of proficiency with technology and their research interests. This can help you adjust how much time is spent on training activities. Additionally, you may integrate different proficiency levels into your curriculum, for instance, allowing advanced students to tackle more complicated projects. In other cases, advanced students may act as mentors to novices in the class.

The resources at the end of the chapter include an example of questions to ask students when beginning an AR/VR project.

As with anything in life, technology and devices will not work perfectly all the time. It can be useful to outline the solutions to frequent problems, errors, or hurdles students may face, ahead of time. This need not be an activity that falls solely on the instructor. Troubleshooting and co-constructing a knowledge base of frequent problems and solutions can be part of the student contributions for the duration of the project. These kinds of activities are especially useful for projects that span longer periods of time or carry over from one group of students to another. The cocreation of knowledge supports the peer-learning model and has been found to be a useful asynchronous activity for students (DiPasquale and Hunter 2022). MediaWiki and Google Docs are effective knowledge management tools with short learning curves (Chu and Kennedy 2011). At Georgia Tech, student research teams made use of wikis and Web-based documents to organize and share frequently asked questions and answers. The information carried over from semester to semester as senior students graduated or left the project and handed off work to incoming students. Building a learning activity such as this into the curriculum not only creates an ongoing knowledge base and shared understanding of the development process, but also saves the students valuable time by providing reference materials for issues that arise frequently. As a result, troubleshooting response time is kept to a minimum. Consider selecting a suitable knowledge management tool before beginning your program.

CONCLUSION

To summarize a few main takeaways of technology solutions, start small by focusing on creating AR/VR/MR content with the resources your organization may already have access to rather than designing and developing from scratch. Test out the use cases and user experience with students for scaling. It is also important to remember that the project is most importantly a vehicle for exploration and experimentation. Students' final products are not as important as what can be gained from the trial-and-error process of learning to use these tools. Semi-structured projects give students flexibility if changes to their project design are needed due to technical issues or limitations. A project can be adjusted in technology solutions, structure, or scope as the students progress.

When trying to find these solutions, don't hesitate to use institutional, community, and online resources to resolve some of the issues your team encounters. If students choose to work in a team, a tool for collaborative projects is Unity's DevOps program (https://unity.com/products/unity-devops/pricing). Ongoing and structured documentation is important, just as it is in coding. Building timely saves and regular documentation into student projects can help both students and instructors get in the habit of evaluating resources and workflow. Some examples include student exit tickets, status reports, and easy-to-fill-out forms.

REFERENCES

Chu, Samuel Kai-Wai, and David M. Kennedy. 2011. "Using online collaborative tools for groups to co-construct knowledge." *Online Information Review.* August 9. https://www.emerald.com/insight/content/doi/10.1108/14684521111161945/full/pdf?title=using-online-collaborative-tools-for-groups-to-coconstruct-knowledge.

ClassVR. n.d. "ClassVR storage and charging." https://www.classvr.com/school-virtual-reality/classroom-case-vr-headset-8/.

DeCristofaro, Christopher, James Hutter, and Nick Tanzi. 2020. *Best technologies for public libraries: Policies, programs, and services.* Santa Barbara, CA: Libraries Unlimited.

DiPasquale, Joshua, and William J. Hunter. 2022. "Fostering productive social interactions using asynchronous activities." Thriving Online: A Guide for Busy Educators. Toronto, ON: Open Library. https://ecampusontario.pressbooks.pub/aguideforbusyeducators/chapter/fostering-productive-social-interactions-using-asynchronous-activities/.

Georgia Tech Library. n.d.a. "Azden wired lavalier." GT Library Gadgets Equipment Lending Catalog. https://libcal.library.gatech.edu/equipment/item/135154.

Georgia Tech Library. n.d.b. "Equipment lending (gadgets)." https://library.gatech.edu/gadgets.

ISTE. 2016. "ISTE standards: Students." https://www.iste.org/standards/iste-standards-for-students.

Mount Vernon School. 2018. "MV students & Dell Alienware officially launch virtual reality lab." April 11. https://mountvernonschool.org/mv-students-dell-alienware-officially-launch-virtual-reality-lab/.

Mount Vernon School. 2020. "Upper school virtual reality students partner with Children's Healthcare of Atlanta." January 15. https://mountvernonschool.org/upper-school-virtual-reality-students-partner-with-childrens-healthcare-of-atlanta/.

Nguyen, Vinh. T., Jung Kwanghee, and Tommy Dang. 2019. "Creating virtual reality and augmented reality development in classroom: Is it a hype?" *2019 IEEE International Conference on Artificial Intelligence and Virtual Reality (AIVR).* 2019: 212–2125. doi: 10.1109/AIVR46125.2019.00045.

Pichman, Brian. 2019. "IT security for libraries part 1: Securing your library." *RAILS: Reaching Across Illinois Library System*, January 21. https://www.railslibraries.info/system/files/Anyone/mtg/135822/IT%20Security%20Part%201%20slides.pdf.

Providence Day School. n.d. "Digital citizenship Providence Day School digital compass." https://pdsdigitalcitizenship.org/.

Richmond, Emily. 2017. "Student-centered learning." *Stanford Center for Opportunity Policy in Education*, June 26. https://edpolicy.stanford.edu/news/articles/1193.

Toller, Alison. 2018. "An inconceivable partnership: Dell said yes." *The Mount Vernon Magazine*, January 11. http://mvmag.pub/2018/01/11/an-inconceivable-partnership/.

Wikipedia. 2022. "List of virtual reality headsets." https://en.wikipedia.org/wiki/Comparison_of_virtual_reality_headsets.

Wikipedia. 2022. "Windows mixed reality." https://en.wikipedia.org/wiki/Windows_Mixed_Reality.

zSpace. n.d. "Introducing the zSpace inspire." https://zspace.com/technology/inspire.

RESOURCES

You know what you have and have determined your long-term goals. Now what tools and technologies will help you implement your project ideas?

Evaluating Your Organization's Strategic Goals and SWOT Analysis

- What is your program's mission statement?

- What are your program's strengths? (internal, positive)

- What are your program's weaknesses? (internal, negative)

- What are your program's opportunities? (external, positive)

____

____

- What are your program's threats? (external, negative)

____

____

____

____

____

Evaluating and Establishing Your Device Collection

- What is the age range of your learners?

____

____

____

____

____

- Will your projects be done for academic credit, extracurricularly, or casually?

____

____

____

____

____

- What is your estimated starting budget?

____

____

____

____

____

- What partnerships are available to augment or extend your existing budget?

- Given the scope of your learners and potential projects, what scale do you estimate for your collection?

Assessing VR Equipment

VR headsets are frequently changing and updating. To get your search started, review this table in Wikipedia to see the status of different products. Note that Wikipedia is crowdsourced, so it's a good idea to corroborate any information you find in this table with external sources. https://en.wikipedia.org/wiki/Comparison_of_virtual_reality_headsets

Evaluating Your Workspace

- What is the size and shape of your workspace?

- Where are your power supply locations?

  ____

  ____

  ____

  ____

  ____

- Where are your data port locations?

  ____

  ____

  ____

  ____

  ____

- Where can your "instructional hub" be located for maximum visibility?

  ____

  ____

  ____

  ____

  ____

- Where could you set up an interactive zone for using the headsets?

  ____

  ____

  ____

  ____

  ____

- How many learners can the space comfortably hold?

  ____

  ____

  ____

____

____

Draw a simple room diagram here for mapping out your power supplies (@), data ports(#), and table/desk (rectangle/circle) locations:

Project Management Concepts for Project-Based Learning

- Clear goals: Realistic and measurable.
- Clear deliverables.
- Outline roles and responsibilities.
- Delegate tasks.
- Involve stakeholders.
- Include regular status updates and milestones.
- Adjust project parameters based on budget requirements.
- Implement a communication plan and regular check-ins.
- Identify strengths, weaknesses, opportunities, and threats—or a risk assessment.
- Have a means of measuring progress.

Starter Questions to Ask Peer Institutions

See the list of questions in the resources for Chapter 5.

Locating 3D Models

- Blocks: Free 3D model making tool. https://vr.google.com/blocks/
- Medium: 3D modeling tool with Oculus. https://www.oculus.com/medium/
- Unity Asset Store. https://assetstore.unity.com/3d

Project Ideas Based on Time Frames

Note: See more example timelines in Chapter 4.

- Long weekend
    - Create a basic immersive environment using a 360 camera and Google Cardboard. Sample project can be found here: https://guides.library.ucsc.edu/DS/Resources/GoogleCardboard

- A few weeks
    - Basic interactive environment with Unity Virtual Tour
        - Concepts addressed: Locomotion, interactions, collisions, and animations
        - Use of pre-created 3D models
        - Unity, Android Studio, Oculus SDK, and JDK
        - Utilize Unity beginning essentials. https://unity.com/learn
        - Assign a few key tutorials from the platform
- Semester or quarter
    - Comprehensive interactive experience with Unity—Chemistry Lab Safety Training
        - Concept addressed: polished storyline about the lab safety protocol, create a virtual scene with lab items from Assets Store, add advanced interaction with items in the lab
        - Unity, Unity Asset Store, create your 3D objects with Blender (optional)
- Full school year
    - Comprehensive research and multiple technical resources—100 Years Campus History through AR Lens
        - Concept addressed: research on campus history and change of landscape, overlay old images of campus on current environment with smartphone, embed brief text explaining the old images
        - Unity, Google Earth API, Android Studio and SDK, Android smartphone

Evaluating Your Cybersecurity

- What cyber- and network security programs are already in place at your institution?

  ____

  ____

- What administrative permissions exist on your VR Lab machines?

- Who is your point person for cybersecurity concerns?

- What digital citizenship programs are already in place at your organization? What would you like to add?

FOUR

Student-Centric Research Projects: Learning Models That Fit Students' Interests and Skills

The previous chapters discussed long-term educational goals for technology-based initiatives, as well as the importance of aligning those goals with your organization's strategic plan and their available technologies. This chapter turns the focus to the projects that you and your students will be working on. It covers how to best integrate emerging technologies into your curriculum, engaging student interests, designing lessons for student skills, and assessment strategies. When conceptualizing a research program or course concepts that utilize a flexible framework, it helps to guide the design by considering the existing educational methods and curriculum in an organization. Ideally, the program you develop and the technologies you choose should enhance and complement the classes, lessons, and teaching philosophies you are already offering at your institution.

One benefit of emerging technologies is that they have the potential to enhance the understanding of a subject through highly immersive experiences that allow students to go beyond passive exploration of topics in a traditional classroom setting. The STEAM (science, technology, engineering, arts, and math) curriculum is one such example. The integration of the sciences and arts that incorporates AR/VR technologies into STEAM education can enrich the learning process and deepen a student's understanding of complex concepts. Learning to use the emerging technology equipment or navigate the required software is highly technical in nature, but the benefit can simultaneously be a large part of artistic storytelling. For instance, while using a VR headset, students can engage with content that is both scientific and artistic in nature. An example might be a VR environment that demonstrates the effects of ocean warming on coral reefs. The experience demonstrates the effects of global warming and pollution that result in a bleaching event. As students explore the virtual landscape, the coral changes color through interactions as they control temperature gauges and virtual trash. One similar VR game is called *Ocean Rift*. This game immerses students in a virtual ocean environment interacting with a variety of marine life. These powerful new technologies not only allow students to experience an immersive learning environment but also empower them to develop educational content that represents their own interests or research in order to share with others.

Effective integration of AR/VR in educational environments happens through process. This applies to two definitions of process. First, the equipment and technologies can best serve students when they are integral to the educational process and go beyond classroom activities that are used exclusively for entertainment value. Second, the process of adapting, failing, and iterating is an integral part of designing and implementing in the AR/VR development life cycle. As you and your students design projects, begin with a semi-structured plan. You may need to modify the original project design along the way; perhaps there will be limits to technologies, skill development, resources, or time that require a new path. Remind yourself and your students that the project plan is a *vessel* for exploration and learning. Students will be building their technical skills, teamwork soft skills, and content-related skills throughout the process.

STUDENT-CENTRIC PROJECT DESIGN

Student-centric programming relies on student buy-in. Students are more likely to have buy-in if the projects they are focused on relate to their personal or social interests. Encouraging the exploration of important topics and causes that connect with them on a personal level motivates students to work on diverse project designs. For example, they might be interested in environmental causes, biological systems, or fashion textiles. In addition to design options, collaboration among students could also fuel the learning experience. Depending on their interests, available resources, and time limits, they could work independently or in groups as they prefer. Allowing the students the flexibility of choosing their own topics puts them in control of the project experience and helps sustain interest and engagement. The collaboration process is often more effective when students can work in small groups. As these small teams work together, teammates can take on specific roles, benefiting the progress of the project overall. This topic will be covered in more detail later in the chapter.

Embracing Student Interests

How might instructors begin to explore their students' interests and inspire their curiosity? A skills or interest survey toward the beginning of the project can help the instructor calibrate the pace of the education to suit the students and improve learning opportunities. It can also help pair them appropriately if group work is preferred. So, when considering student-centric research, getting to know the students is a top priority. In the resources section at the end of Chapter 2, we have an example of a skills survey and probing questions you can modify and use at your own institution to get students started in the right direction. Survey tools such as Qualtrics can be used to gather, store, and anonymize data when needed. However, the key takeaway is that there are several main categories to focus on in the questionnaire and critical information to gather that could be helpful when advising students on their project proposals or concepts. Examples of relevant topics to pursue with students include previous experience with these technologies, relevant coding or 3D modeling experience, general college major, research or personal interests, time constraints, and available time for team meetings. Consider sharing some of the results with everyone in the class to provide full transparency on desirable skill sets. This will help the students leverage each other's strengths and be aware of potential constraints early in the process.

Classes that are centered around original student concepts would begin with students researching topics of interest and constructing their project ideas. Ultimately the students will be developing a proposal to submit to instructors. During this initial research and ideation process, they determine if they want to work with others or independently. Once a group has reached consensus and identified a suitable topic, instructors would work with them to tailor the project scope to the time and material constraints. Take, for instance, a group of students who have a general interest in fiber or textile studies as it relates to fashion. The team might want to make a full haute couture collection and expo center in a virtual environment. To adjust scope, instructors might suggest the team first create a single virtual costume after finding or modeling different fabrics and materials. The effort and time commitment of creating the first model would give the team a realistic estimate of the time needed and adjust their collection size accordingly. As the development progresses, if time permits, students could scale up the project by adding more garments and accessories, and search for existing 3D models of an interior theater, catwalk, or storefront to display their creations.

Team Building, Personal Connections, and Icebreakers

For students who will be working closely and collaborating on a technical project, it is beneficial to develop meaningful connections early in the process. Instructors can assist in fostering peer interactions. Personal connections are just as important as understanding interests, skill sets, and technical expertise. In addition to a simple survey or questionnaire, some in-person or online activities can assist students in connecting with their class peers. Robb and Shellenbarger (2021) found that "Students who develop connections with faculty and peers early in a course have a sense of group cohesiveness, feel comfortable communicating with faculty and peers, and are more likely to be motivated to engage in course content" (Robb and Shellenbarger 2021). One technique for building trust and forming connections is incorporating team-building activities and icebreakers early into the research class process. Initial icebreaker activities that focus solely on getting to know the student's individual personality and interests can facilitate learning. The sample icebreakers listed here are variations on "getting to know you" activities.

See the resources at the end of the chapter for sample diagrams to go along with some of these icebreaker activities.

- *Bingo.* In this activity, the instructor creates bingo cards with descriptions for each square on the card. Students connect with other students to find out who matches up with the descriptions on the cards. This gives the students a structured mechanism for discussion and an opportunity to get to know one another. Descriptions could include general topics such as favorite foods or traveling experiences. However, on the cards you could also include descriptions specific to activities that might be relevant to the class, such as preferred operating systems, experience with certain software, graphic art skills, or photography skills. This activity can be adapted for in-person or online learning. Students can also submit description ideas ahead of time in their initial questionnaire. Instructors then gather those descriptions and later incorporate them into the bingo card.

- *Interview: Pairs.* Keeping things simple is always a good rule of thumb. For both online classes and in-person classes, having students chat with each other in pairs and then introduce the student they were paired with to the rest of the class is a simple yet effective way to promote peer interactions early in the process. Provide some structure for the activity such as four key questions to incorporate into the interview activity: (1) Name, pronouns, major, where they are from; (2) Hidden talents or sources of pride; (3) Interests; (4) Objectives or goals in taking the class. Interviews can be adapted as an in-person activity that has students moving around the classroom or an online activity with breakout rooms.
- *Best Class/Worst Class.* Another activity that can foster connections among students in a class and between students and their instructors is an activity that prompts them to share some of their best classes and worst classes. Students are asked to share what they consider to be one of their most positive class experiences, along with one that they didn't find enriching. Give them a few minutes to write their ideas down on paper, and then each person goes around and shares their educational memories. Students will likely relate to each other's negative and positive experiences, while instructors can use the activity to reflect on their own pedagogy.
- *What Do You Hope to Learn?* At the heart of most icebreaker activities is getting to know the personalities and interests of participants better. One of the main takeaways from an icebreaker in an educational setting is what an individual hopes to learn or gain through their participation. At the very least, an easy activity to get people talking to each other is the one thing everyone has in common: the class! Simply asking people what they hope to take away from their experience can shed light on personalities and interests and will ultimately begin personal connections.

SELF-REGULATED LEARNING

Self-regulated learning allows students to have more control over their learning journey. Students and teachers become partners in designing learning objectives and developing an appropriate framework for educational goals.

Self-Regulated Learning and Teamwork

Self-regulated learning is a cyclical process. Students will plan for a task, visualize their project goals, monitor aspects of their own performance, adjust their goals if necessary, and finally reflect on the outcome (Zumbrunn, Tadlock, and Roberts 2011). As they reflect on the effectiveness of their planned strategies at milestone points throughout the semester or project duration, they will adjust their implementation methods and adapt. Dumford and Miller (2018) write that "Academic behaviors, including the use of strategies for self-regulated learning, quantitative reasoning, activities that promote higher-order thinking, and reflective and integrative learning, can increase content knowledge as well as overall cognitive processing and are all linked to various aspects of achievement and success."

Self-regulated learning is at the crux of the emerging technologies research classes piloted at the Georgia Tech Library. The library instructors provided a proposal framework that the students used to craft their own goals and objectives for the class. This proposal included an expected timeline, key milestones, regular status reports, required resources, and overall objectives. The class collectively was focused on one main objective; however, in order to reach this goal, they often broke up into groups. Tracks or sub teams were often formed through student interests and skills. In some classes, they would self-select themes or tracks of study based on their interests. For instance, if some students wanted to focus solely on creating 3D models, they would select the modeling track. If visual communication was of particular interest, a student might choose to work with the graphic design track. Students who self-select into a track would work with other students who selected that same track. The tracks were structured by library instructors in such a way that these subgroups came together to produce a common project goal. These tracks or sub-teams were expected to communicate with each other and coordinate work efforts toward the overall project goals. Whether through track selection or the project proposals, the students are in control of their action plan and time management. Throughout the implementation phase, self-reflection activities are built into the timeline at key points, giving the students opportunity for course correction and project modification.

Collaboration and teamwork are essential skills preparing students for work environments. However, in the educational setting, working in teams can be both rewarding and challenging for them. Students have competing academic priorities and disjointed schedules that do not always make it easy logistically to collaborate in the same way you might in a traditional working environment. As a result, unless team projects are effectively facilitated and organized by the instructor, these course collaborations can be a source of frustration for the students, thus detracting from the project learning objectives. Hansen lists ten key strategies for successfully structuring team projects that will benefit student-centric research projects (2006):

- Emphasizing the importance and relevance of teams and teamwork
- Teaching team development and teamwork skills
- Conducting team-building exercises for cohesive groups
- Determining method of team formation
- Assigning a reasonable workload and establishing clear goals
- Requiring team members to have specific and assigned roles
- Providing some class time for team meetings
- Requesting interim reports and other feedback points
- Requiring individual team members to keep personal contributions file
- Using detailed peer evaluations as a part of grading team effort

Integral to the success of the Georgia Tech Library research class was integrating best practices for team dynamics into the project framework and the grading criteria. Team formation was often a result of student track selection. Each track has its own criteria and expectations for deliverables. Rather than being randomly placed together or forced to self-select other team members, students were strategically placed together based on the information they provided through their initial questionnaire and their academic goals. Skill sets were equally distributed through the teams, often falling into specific roles. In the Georgia Tech framework, half the scheduled classes were used as all-team meetings with instructors. The other half of classes gave students time on their schedules to meet with each other. All-team meetings that included the instructors required the students to report on any progress to everyone, in addition to their weekly status reports that were submitted online. A large part of the final grade required students to self-reflect on their own contributions to the project work, as well as the contributions of their peers. The final report designated a section for self-reflection. The reflection covered both the final deliverables and the project process.

When taking these ten key strategies into consideration, it will be critical to raise the students' awareness of the importance of teamwork. Improving individual *and* team metacognition for both course content and the project process can improve knowledge transfer and collaborative problem-solving skills. Metacognition is described as the awareness of one's own intellectual reasoning alongside the ability to consciously monitor and control these processes (Schraw 1998). Metacognitive ability has been shown to be beneficial in communication skills and complex problem-solving (Wiltshire et al. 2014). McCarthy and Garavan (2008) state: "Although team members will have individual perspectives and cognition, it is a collective perspective or a collective knowledge structure at the team level that guides the direction of the team." Therefore, in addition to providing students with metacognitive prompts for learning the hard skills associated with the technology used in developing AR/VR, equal attention should be given to how the team will build collective knowledge.

When emphasizing the importance and relevance of teamwork, introducing students to concepts integral to project management is one approach that can assist them in developing a cohesive group dynamic. Key project management concepts to consider integrating into your curriculum might be managing scope and timeline, defining roles, drafting use cases, managing change within the project, and defining deliverables. It is important for the instructor to develop an effective framework that sets students up for success. For instance, having team milestones predefined and presenting regular status updates provide students with a mechanism for communicating progress and receiving feedback. When students are required to submit a team contract or proposal early in the semester, goals and deliverables are clearly defined, agreed on, and open to discussion and input from all. This also allows instructors who are in essence project managers the ability to assist in coordinating team roles. Project instructors should review proposals, sign off when approved, adjust resources where needed, and ensure students understand what is expected and how deliverables will be evaluated at the end of the required timeline.

Best practices for teamwork conclude by giving students the opportunity to reflect on their learning journey. This reflection can take the form of a weekly journal, a final reflection document, or other means of documenting personal contributions along with lessons learned. It is important to have students discuss the contributions of others as well. In the absence of traditional project oversight as one might find in a job setting, there must be a mechanism in place that keeps students accountable to each other. Instructors should make sure to discuss team member contributions at any weekly check-in meetings. There are also peer evaluation mechanisms in place that allow students to rank each other, but also to account for how much time they spend collaborating with each student. Scores are weighted heavier for students who work together more frequently, since projects are often set up in sub-teams. Students also self-grade themselves using an instructor-created rubric at the midpoint of the project.

As noted by Schraw (1998), "Extended practice and reflection play crucial roles in the construction of metacognitive knowledge and regulatory skills. This is especially true when students are given regular opportunities to reflect on one's successes and failures." Providing metacognitive prompts for the students at various stages in their project development allows for further refinement and behavioral adjustments in team planning, team knowledge building, team knowledge sharing, and team reflexivity (Wiltshire et al. 2014).

The following list of metacognitive prompts can be adapted for team projects involving AR/VR:

Team Planning Prompts:

- What tasks and activities are a priority to you, and what is the least important?
- What roles are defined in this team? What is each person individually responsible for?
- What is the plan for accomplishing the goals you have set for yourself?
- If someone cannot complete their portion of the work, do you have a backup plan?
- What types of resources do all team members need access to?

Team Knowledge Building and Sharing Prompts:

- What knowledge or information is critical for you to know?
- What knowledge or information is critical for your teammates to know?

- What information will you need to share with others?
- How is the information required to complete this project interconnected?

Team Reflection Prompts:

- Was the team effectively organized?
- What errors prevented you from reaching your goals?
- Were the team communication channels an asset to learning?

Self-Regulated Learning and Libraries

The concept of self-regulated learning is related to the concept of "self-directed learning" that is referenced in the ACRL (Association for College and Research Libraries) Framework for Information Literacy for Higher Education (2015). Information literacy is described as "the set of integrated abilities encompassing the reflective discovery of information, the understanding of how information is produced and valued, and the use of information in creating new knowledge and participating ethically in communities of learning" (ACRL 2015). Metaliteracy is broadly considered "the ability to evaluate information for its bias, reliability, and credibility and apply them in the context of production and sharing of knowledge" (Mackey and Jacobson 2011). ACRL states, "Metaliteracy demands behavioral, affective, cognitive, and metacognitive engagement with the information ecosystem" (ACRL 2015). The importance of self-reflection in student learning is described in the ACRL framework as depending on "these core ideas of metaliteracy, with special focus on metacognition, or critical self-reflection, as crucial to becoming more self-directed in that rapidly changing ecosystem." Woven throughout this framework for education in academic libraries is the idea that librarians should be collaborating with academic partners on pedagogical research and involving students in that research.

The ACRL framework emphasizes metacognition as an integral part of library instruction. However, as mentioned by Houtman, the framework doesn't clearly address the implementation of these concepts (2015). Self-regulated learning and its core elements are one path forward and an approach librarians can take for promoting students' self-awareness and learning skills. The shift to a learner-centered approach in teaching and education, as opposed to a content-driven approach, is not entirely new to libraries. When students search for and select library resources to perform research, the process itself incorporates self-reflection and self-directed practices. Some of these self-regulated practices may include choosing or changing to appropriate controlled vocabulary, determining relevancy of research findings to a chosen topic, and identifying research synergies through the selective use of metadata. The research process by nature is self-regulated and iterative as the student researchers reflect on their process and adjust, as needed. Librarians can mitigate student frustration by providing a supportive environment through scaffolded instruction and consultation. Informing library users about best practices for search strategies and resource evaluation can help them refine this self-driven process. As Simons states, "Self-directed learning is a social-interactive, contextual, constructive, self-regulated and reflective process" (2000).

Libraries at their core are interdisciplinary. Librarians frequently work across disciplines to identify resources that benefit research that touches multiple departments and research areas. This environment complements the learner-centered approach of self-regulated learning. Students are encouraged to reflect on their own research and other related work through the lens of multiple disciplines. When students participate in library-led research initiatives, the library has the opportunity of going beyond the functions of information repository and basic retrieval to becoming an incubator of cross-curricular ideas. Much of the research on self-regulated learning in libraries has been focused on how we implement that approach within the context of information literacy. As libraries redefine our ideas of what library resources are and how libraries can support research and learning, we should extend our ideas of self-regulated learning into the realm of emerging technologies. Providing students with the framework to not only design their own cross-disciplinary research projects, but also with mechanisms for the students to reflect on how they are learning is promoting metacognition in the AR/VR development life cycle. When libraries can effectively integrate reflective activities into research and instruction, this increases both student engagement and the students' synthesis of information.

Students benefit from interdisciplinary research opportunities using emerging technologies offered by libraries. First, libraries offer them access to the hardware. Through library lending programs and specialized labs, emerging technology such as VR/MR headsets, controllers, as well as media creation and development workstations are made available to students who might not otherwise have access to these resources due to financial or logistical constraints. Libraries act as equalizers by providing access to advanced technologies and software regardless of background. Within this low-stakes environment where grades are often not always emphasized, students who might not otherwise have a way to experiment with these technologies in their own designated major are given an opportunity to learn more about them. Second, librarians provide learning resources to accompany the hands-on experiences. For example, when students are first conceptualizing "what is possible" in a AR/VR research class, librarians can assist them by showing them how to access case studies, relevant tutorials, or research studies that facilitate visualizing their final project ideas. Furthermore, librarians who specialize in emerging technologies can guide students in the appropriate use of open-source software, applications, and plug-ins. This includes not only the use of software but also how to vet and research software in order to select the appropriate tool. Introducing students to industry-standard publications can be one avenue for software or hardware evaluation as well as exposure to the latest technology trends. In conclusion, students gain experiences beyond their disciplinary silos by participating in research projects led through a library environment. By implementing a pedagogical approach that incorporates self-regulated learning, librarians are ideally positioned to design interdisciplinary educational initiatives that introduce students to emerging technologies.

INSTRUCTORS AS MENTORS AND PROJECT MANAGERS

Instructors can assist students in locating appropriate resources, designing learning activities, and creating roles that align with their project goals. Scaffolding course work and providing expectations for critical team roles is a key starting point.

Scaffolding Student Projects

Designed as a project-based learning experience, the VR Research Section at Georgia Tech adopts a scaffolding approach to help students break the project into manageable learning activities and succeed. Scaffolding is considered an effective instructional tool for student success in traditional learning environments (Palincsar and Brown 1984). A recent meta-analysis shows that scaffolding "could be effective to the learning outcomes in digital game-based learning" (Cai and Mao 2022). This study also demonstrated scaffolding techniques were more effective on elementary school and college students than secondary school students. This approach is also supported by MacLeod and van der Veen's (2020) research with a class of interdisciplinary students whose work was similar to that of Georgia Tech's research class. They collected data from students of a project-based class over two years and concluded that their course with the scaffolding approach gives most students a meaningful learning experience. Over the course of two years of iterative improvements, students appreciated the project-driven learning approach more and more with each iteration.

Learning experiences that include AR/VR research have multiple layers of content and numerous challenges involved. Using a scaffolding approach can help students manage the process, break the work into groups of small tasks and tackle them. Cai and Mao (2022) pointed out in their research that to get the most out of the scaffolding approach, the problems need to be structured with students' background, coursework, and technical skills in mind, which incorporates the idea of student-centric learning as previously discussed. For the Georgia Tech research section that focused on AR/VR, student project designs took into consideration not only the students' varying skill levels but also the different course credit commitments, as students can take one to three credits for the class based on their personal learning goals. Librarian instructors mentor students based on their academic credits in order to scale their project design appropriately for their course workload. For instance, students enrolled for three credits would be encouraged to create a larger and possibly more challenging project than students enrolled in one credit. For students with large projects and intensive coding, the instructors make sure to build in time to help them learn the basics of the technical tools needed, most often Unity, if they didn't have previous experience. Students are required to follow some online tutorials and create basic content at the end of each tutorial. This happens in the first five weeks. After this initial phase of hands-on activities, students gain more confidence and are ready to start working independently or in groups on their own projects. Depending on the complexity of the projects and an individual's focus, some of them will need to learn specific tools or skills, such as 3D scanning with their choice of scanner and 3D modeling with an open-source tool, such as Blender.

There are three steps to the success of scaffolding in project-based learning: the problem needs to be clearly stated, could be decomposed to smaller tasks, and could be solved with the course elements (MacLeod and van der Veen 2020). For Georgia Tech's research class, the team went through iterative methods to clarify these three points. The problem was clearly identified during the design phase and stated in students' project proposals. Addressing the problem or challenge was then parsed into different phases or specific tasks. Ultimately, classes of this nature encourage an ongoing dialogue with the students about their development process. In this case, experimentation and failure are encouraged as learning activities. While the final product is important, what is more meaningful is the student's reflection on the process.

The way that you scaffold your program should be tailored to your audience, be it higher ed, K–12, or community programs. To acclimate to the classroom culture that you've already established and the working age group, some students might need more scaffolding or project guidance than others. Younger students or students new to a project-based classroom might need more structure and curriculum-driven content. This is especially true when working with technologies like AR/VR/MR, with which students are starting from scratch learning how to use, edit, and build virtual environments. Students that have worked on art or technical projects before, or students that have more familiarity with the project-based learning process, are more likely to be able to succeed in such open-concept projects, with the teacher acting as a project facilitator rather than content instructor. Customizing the guidance and communicating frequently are the key to scaffolding open-structured project designs.

Defining Team Roles

Key to the success of managing a technology-intensive team project is the concept of roles. As mentioned earlier, a major component for successfully structuring a team project is requiring team members to have specific and assigned roles in the research (Hansen 2006). If not directly assigning roles, instructors can provide guidance for student self-selection through a skills survey or self-evaluation at the beginning of the project. By really digging deep and exploring what the student hopes to gain from the project, library instructors can assist in crafting roles and tasks for individual members of the team. When assessing roles, instructors should consider existing student skills and existing student interests, which aren't always the same. Designing a mechanism to differentiate between what a student is adept at and what they may not be skilled at but hope to gain from the experience should happen early in the project timeline. For instance, a student may be skilled in coding and could contribute significantly to this area, but they would like to expand their knowledge base and experiences into the realm of exploring resources for 3D modeling. Finding a balance between these two is something that will enrich the student's learning experience. This can be accomplished through structured partnerships or subgroups. As an example, partnering students together with skills that complement each other is one way to strike balance. A student who is already adept at coding such as C# could be paired with another student who wants to learn more about C#. Students who are interested in 3D modeling could be paired with individuals in the project who have some experience there. When the instructor looks at the students' skills in the class as a whole, they can assist in partnering students or providing them with appropriate mentors. In this way, students are both providing expertise to their peers and gaining new learning experiences themselves that contribute to the collective knowledge of the team. The design of a skills and interest survey or assessment tool at the beginning of the project is a critical step in developing the project framework.

Roles and peer learning within the context of group research and projects are multifactorial. Another element to effective teamwork and successful collaboration is building social connections. A project support structure that includes contracts, roles, and peer evaluations is much less effective in strengthening social skills and teamwork in the absence of team-building exercises and other activities that foster socioemotional interactions (Chang and Brickman 2018). Earlier we mentioned that icebreakers and similar activities provide opportunities for meaningful interactions between students and team members; this also can build trust and a sense of belonging. This in turn means students are more likely to be motivated to engage in course content (Robb and Shellenbarger 2021). Therefore, instructors should go beyond activities that simply match up student skill sets or craft deadlines. The role of the instructor should also be one of creating community. For Georgia Tech, this included the creation of VR game nights and meetups. Outside of the context of academic classes, students from across campus, including those in the library's VR research class, were invited to come and explore the VR games and resources available at the library. This provided a vehicle for students with a general interest in emerging technologies to get to know each other personally outside of the pressures and expectations of classwork. It is in some ways easier for a library with a designated service point devoted to AR/VR to facilitate this type of community-building activity. Social support and community cohesion will complement the research classwork. For a traditional classroom experience in a specific department or discipline, with no associated service point or lab, this kind of community-building activity might be more difficult. In a traditional learning environment, the social aspect of the classroom experience can end when the class ends, but libraries with an active service point can continue the sense of community and the learning experience beyond the bounds of the semester or project time frame. Therefore, libraries that can incorporate AR/VR services alongside their instructional programming are an ideal setting for these team-oriented research classes.

Developing a framework for a VR research class that includes roles will require continued input and guidance from instructors. As students submit their project roles, instructors should make suggestions and adjustments before those roles are solidified and finalized. Chang and Brickman found that if students were left to self-select roles completely, even with basic roles predefined by the instructors, without guidance and feedback, "students fail to use role assignment and group contracts to their fullest" (2018). Without meaningful feedback from instructors, students viewed the team framework as an obstruction to the collaboration process. Chang and Brickman also noted this had the potential to "erode the sense of trust needed for the social interactions required for social interdependence" (2018).

Emphasizing time management skills as appropriate to specific roles will be an important component of the work. With time constraints in mind, it will be important to distribute time-intensive tasks among several team members rather than having that work shouldered by only one or two students. One mechanism for tracking time distribution and encouraging transparency between team members is having the students fill out a simple online weekly log that indicates in a sentence or two what the student did and how much time they spent on it. A simple time log can also assist instructors in determining if a student is getting bogged down or spending too much time on a particular research activity, allowing the instructor to intervene and advise.

The following list includes example roles for a team project utilizing AR/VR technologies. This is not an exhaustive list but is indicative of some key roles you may want to consider when designing your research project. You will also want to consider the age and skill level of the students and adjust accordingly. Presenting ideas such as this to the students can assist them in creating their own roles and workflow as team formation begins.

- **Coding and Programmer Role**
    - Coding skills in C++ or C#; these are especially useful when using Unity
    - Swift, JavaScript
    - Object-oriented programming concepts
    - SDK concepts
- **Media Creator/Camera Operator Role**
    - Filming and using a 360 camera
    - Volumetric capture-camera operators, green screen
- **3D Modeling Role: 3D Assets**
    - Knowledge of the asset store, use of pre-created assets
    - Modeling and texturing with Blender
    - Maya, Cinema4D
- **Audio Engineer Role: Music, Soundtracks**
    - Knowledge of audio production (microphones, mixers)
    - Audio editing in Adobe Audition or Audacity
- **Graphic Designer/Technical Artist Role**
    - Mockups
    - Graphic creation in the Adobe Creative Suite
- **Scripting, Storyboarding, Writer Role**
- **Researcher Role**

To avoid misunderstandings later in the process, roles should be defined clearly at the outset of the project. Clear roles, with clear interconnections, allow students to know what to contribute, who to ask for assistance, and how to manage their time. Positive engagement leads to positive outcomes. When students have distinct roles, this gives them the opportunity to showcase their unique contributions to the collective team project. One way to do this is coordinating a public or community presentation event at the conclusion of the project that allows students to share their work, both individually and as a team.

DESIGNING PROJECTS AND LESSONS

In this section, we will review strategies to consider while developing projects and lessons. After covering ideas and mindsets to use when developing an overall project, the next sections will cover the format of individual lessons and how to select student milestones. The last sections will go over strategies for student assessment and reflection.

Project Structure

While the education models for AR/VR/MR are student-driven, strong scaffolding from the instructors can help students learn and apply their learning more effectively. Key areas to structure time for include play, practice, formal worktime, growth/iteration, reflection, and presentation.

Libraries are an ideal environment to introduce the element of play into education. Time to play with the materials can include introductory activities that help students learn what aspects, tools, or team roles in the class they are interested in. Exposure to different AR or VR projects and different types of 3D recording and modeling software can help students identify which qualities they are most inspired by and which roles they feel most aligned with. Small assignments allow students to familiarize themselves with the software and hardware tools before designing and embarking on self-driven projects. This realm of "play" ties into the area of "practice," where students can learn and develop their skills on a smaller scale, or on a less intense project, so that they build their personal confidence and technical competence.

A large portion of the project will include formal worktime and iteration. This section should begin with formal proposals where student teams think through all aspects of the project they wish to create. The more detailed the proposal, the more accurately the team and instructor(s) can estimate needed assets and time allotment. As mentioned, these proposals should begin mapping out how many scenes the project will include. Students may choose to use a storyboard format that includes an image and detailed notes (see sample in Chapter 7). Each scene should have notes for the content that will be found or created for that scene, including images, video, audio, 3D scans, 3D models, or some combination thereof. The descriptions should also include how the viewer/user will access each scene and what interactions the team would like to add within each scene.

After reviewing their proposal and editing it into a plan, the students can set milestones for the given worktime allotted to the project. More information about milestones can be found in a subsequent section in this chapter. It's useful for students to be flexible and willing to adapt their project plan during implementation, if their timeline calls for it. This time for iteration and growth can be helpful following technical issues or user-testing feedback.

The last portion of the project structure is time for reflection, presentation, and archiving. This section gives teams a distinct goal and deadline to guide their project creation. At the end of the project, reflection takes the form of a project report where students discuss the design, goals, implementation, and challenges. Although as alluded to earlier, reflection is also a component that is woven throughout the entire project timeline. Students can present their final project to the class or community. Depending on the type of projects, students may also host an interim playtesting session earlier in the project structure, which also gives an opportunity for feedback and iteration before the project is completed. Archiving consists of saving and preserving both the project and design solutions for the long term. Reserve time to save the project and assets to an accessible location. Students should also have a formal way to notate any major technical challenges and troubleshooting solutions they encountered during the project.

Here are example semester guides that can be adapted to semester-length classes, which are roughly 15–17-week periods with 2–5 contact hours per week. If a course is a year long, the first semester could include multiple smaller projects and the second one or two longer projects. Quarter systems, summer programs, and alternative schedules can stretch or shorten the timescale to better meet those time allotments.

Example Semester Guide with Multiple Projects (15–17 Weeks)

- Week 1–3: Introduction to curriculum, classmates, and software
- Week 4: First small project to show proficiency with software
- Week 5: Second small project to build on skills learned in first project
- Week 6–7: Longer third project that continues to build on skills
- Week 8/Midterms: Presentation, playtesting, internal class feedback on third project
- Week 9: Project teams assigned and begin design planning for final project

- Week 10–12: Project teams pitch designs for implementation on VR devices
- Week 13–15: Teams build final project. Iteration and instructor support
- Week 16–17: Community playtest event and feedback for final project

Example Semester-Long Project Guide (15–17 Weeks)

- Week 1–3: Introduction to curriculum, classmates, and software
- Week 4: Project teams assigned and begin design planning
- Week 5: Project teams pitch designs for implementation on VR devices
- Week 6–8: Teams build first draft of project
- Week 9/Midterms: Practice, troubleshoot, and playtest internally with feedback
- Week 10–12: Teams continue to build project. Iteration and instructor support
- Week 13–15: Continued building, iteration, and instructor support
- Week 16–17: Community playtest event and feedback

Components of a Lesson Plan

Lesson plans, formal guides to projects, can help instructors clarify their goals and student learning objectives at the beginning of a project. Like many of the other aspects we have covered so far, a lesson plan is a flexible document that benefits from iteration and adjustment with each successive run of the project. These lesson plans are especially helpful when creating introductory projects that teach students how to use the hardware and software that will be important components of their independent projects. Different instructors and different disciplines will use variations on a lesson plan format. In general, there are seven sections to cover.

First, identify the overview or purpose of the project. Describe briefly what the project is about. Like a thesis statement in an essay, the purpose can provide direction as students develop a project, and it can be refined as the project develops. This section might also include a guiding and conceptual "essential question" that is meant to stimulate students' thoughts and inquiries.

Second, identify the specific objectives for students. For this section, instructors can identify what students should be learning as they complete the project. These objectives might include specific facts, types of technical skills, interpersonal skills, or how to implement conceptual processes.

Next in the lesson plan are education standards customized by subject and grade level. Depending on your institution and grant status, these standards can be vital to crafting an effective lesson plan. The next section will share some examples of use cases for applying education standards.

Fourth, depending on the age level of your students, the lesson plan might include a list of important vocabulary words that students should be able to use properly. The vocabulary will show up in their classwork, discussions, reflections, and exhibition materials.

Fifth, the lesson plan will elaborate on the materials students need for the project. Consider practicing a dry run to estimate the supplies your students will need and the time it will take to complete the project. (Depending on student efficiency and your own familiarity/ease with the content or technology, double or triple the time it takes you to complete the project to approximate student worktime.) When beginning a project, list everything the students could possibly need, including connective wires, chargers, storage devices, account log-ins, and software installations. Note if materials are shared among students or are used per student. This section can be adjusted as you work through the steps of the actual activity later on.

Verification holds the sixth position. This section covers the ways you will check for students' understanding. Here you can list ways that you will identify if students are following along with instruction, understanding the materials, and reaching their learning objectives. Verifying students' progress forms key milestones in the project's cycle. A future section will cover some ways to structure milestones and help keep students on track for success.

Following the verification section is an enumeration of the steps of the actual activity. For the first time students run a project, it can be useful to detail each and every step. One strategy to format the steps of the project is to consider the major events or milestones of the project, as identified in the fifth section, and then create subheadings with the detailed tasks necessary underneath each of those events.

The final section of the lesson plan covers assessment, reflection, and exhibitions. Here instructors identify what the final output of the project will be and what materials will be shared with the instructors, the class, or the community. A future section in this chapter will go into more detail about assessment strategies and rubrics. In general, clear rubrics can help both instructors and the students prioritize learning objectives and time management. These documents should be provided to students at the beginning of a class. Reflection opportunities help students process and integrate their learning. These reflections might be written or recorded. Lastly, the exhibition component might be an internal critique among peers in the class or an open day in the lab where you invite the community to experience the projects. Exhibitions are great opportunities for engagement and connection.

Structuring Milestones

When designing course activities that provide learners with experience in AR/VR/MR technologies, library instructors aim to strike a balance between a structured framework and a flexible path. If students are left largely on their own to plan a timeline for fundamentals, design, and prototyping, the learning experience could be a source of frustration. This is because students could be inclined to get bogged down on issues they can't solve; it is the responsibility of the instructor to recognize the tendency to hyper focus on the negative and intervene if they see a student is getting offtrack. Therefore, instructors should provide clearly defined milestones, require regular status updates, and help define the learning outcomes for the project.

Students should spend enough time on fundamentals that the initial learning activities support their design ideas, giving them enough knowledge to implement their project concepts. However, instructors should emphasize that the stages and steps of the course or project do not necessarily have to be completed in succession and they are not mutually exclusive. For instance, without guidance or key checkpoints, the early stages of familiarizing oneself with the hardware and software could easily take up the first half of a 15-week semester. However, instructors can encourage some overlapping steps and stages, and perhaps some design work is being done in parallel with learning the fundamentals.

Setting up milestones in cooperation with the students serves as a control mechanism for the learning journey. Milestones will assist all involved in evaluating if a project concept is feasible within the overall time available or if adjustment of the scope is needed. Milestones also assist students in dividing the tasks, managing and modifying subtasks in a timely manner. Overall, milestones give students more agency over the process through effective time management. Principles of project management can be very useful in this case. For instance, introducing the concept of a change request or a resource request. Allowing the process to be an accurate representation of how a typical project workflow might occur will give the students valuable experience. Providing students with the appropriate language to make use of these project management tools will assist them in proposing realistic milestones.

Milestones can be selected from any of these key stages or steps:

- Introduction of project parameters and requirements
- Exploration of case studies for inspiration
- Understanding the language of project management (index of terms)
- Submission of proposal
- Getting to know team members—identifying tasks and assigning roles
- Fundamentals: familiarization with resources
    - Exploring and playing AR/VR games or experiences
    - Understanding the language—key terms to know
- Fundamentals: software, basic tutorials, or learning exercises
    - Example Unity tutorials
    - Making a basic shape in Blender
    - Using a 360 camera
- Implementation and testing stages
    - Identification of scenes or environments
    - Selecting what assets and materials will need to be created
    - Assigning and creating assets, scenes, or environments
    - Playtesting within team or with peers
    - Editing based on playtesting feedback
- Final project showcase
- Reflections—woven throughout the project timeline from start to finish.

Student-Centric Research in Higher Ed

The design philosophy at Georgia Tech is to encourage students to work on their passion projects. In the past four years, we have seen students working on a wide variety of projects, including an immersive campus tour, a virtual scavenger hunt in Sweden, a creative anaglyph poster campaign, and meditation in a virtual environment. Students begin with breaking down a rough project idea into smaller components under the guidance of the instructors; they then budget time for each task, and finally implement and adjust the project throughout the semester.

Project designs vary. Some simply use images with 3D format or special effects built into them, while others require more complicated content and formatting, which involves learning the use of professional editing tools. Some of the most important tools we saw students use in the past are Unity and Blender. Unity is the game engine where students import all materials to compile into a game; Blender is a 3D graphic editing tool for students to create or edit their own 3D models.

To get students started with implementation, especially those who didn't have rich experience with these tools, we devote a few weeks at the beginning of the semester for students to watch and follow tutorials of these tools, followed by a project design proposal. Take the virtual Georgia Tech tour as an example (demo video available at https://smartech.gatech.edu/handle/1853/60493). It delivers an immersive virtual campus visit guided by BuzzBot, a robot inspired by the Georgia Tech mascot Buzz (Figure 4-1). The project started with creating a virtual environment as the landing spot for viewers when they started the tour; they chose a few campus landmark

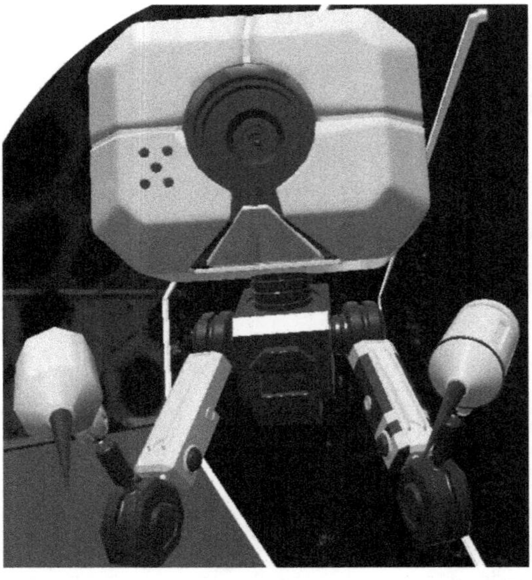

Figure 4-1 BuzzBot from the Georgia Tech Virtual Campus Tour

locations to include in the tour, with each location having some information embedded to help viewers learn more about the current scene. Students utilized a 360 camera for some of the images used in the project. To prepare students for project implementation, it is advisable to have the project design plan as detailed as possible.

See sample storyboard and scene planning forms in the resources at the end of the chapter.

Some questions students should be able to answer with the design proposals are:

1. How many scenes do they want to include in their projects?
2. What is the input of each scene, whether an image, video, audio, 3D scans, virtual scene created in Unity, or a combination of multiple input?
3. For each scene, do they need to create the scene and objects, or can they have it available somewhere?
4. What interactions do they want to add?

Given this list, some terms to be familiar with are as follows. "Scenes contain the objects of your game. They can be used to create a main menu, individual levels, and anything else. Think of each unique Scene file as a unique level. In each Scene, you will place your environments, obstacles, and decorations, essentially designing and building your game in pieces" (Unity Documentation 2021). "An Interaction represents a specific input pattern. For example, a hold is an Interaction that requires a Control to be held for at least a minimum amount of time" (Unity Manual 2021).

To implement this project, students first used free assets from the Unity asset store to create a fictional landing space called the Georgia Tech Space Station. In the station, students incorporated historical photographs from the institute archives to educate users on Georgia Tech history. To add to that, students also selected a RAT hat from the archives collection to create a 3D model to display in the station. A RAT hat is a Georgia Tech tradition traced back to the early twentieth century, when freshmen were required to wear a hat with "F" on it representing "freshmen" for the whole first year.

From the station, viewers can teleport to one of the selected locations on campus, including Tech Tower, the Stadium, Clough building (a lab building name after retired Georgia Tech president G. Wayne Clough), and so on. Each tour site on campus was imported in the game as a 3D image to give viewers an immersive panorama view. After adding all selected locations, students then proceeded to determine how to navigate to different sites, and how much interaction to build into each site. BuzzBot guides viewers around the station and enters the control room where viewers can teleport to other campus sites. To enter the control room, BuzzBot needs to use a key card that is a replication of the Georgia Tech campus ID card. As for interaction with the scenes, the initial design also had video and audio effects, and possible interaction with avatars of Georgia Tech characters built in. However, due to the project scale, the multimedia content was removed from the final delivery.

During implementation, there could be setbacks due to the time limits or technological challenges. One example of a challenge on the virtual tour project was the 3D scan of the RAT cap. The students' initial design was to create a 3D model of the hat to place in the space station. The idea was that when viewers wander around in the space station, the hat could be picked up and inspected; viewers or the BuzzBot may even be able to try it on. To create this model, the students needed a high-resolution 3D scanner to scan the inside and outside of it. We were able to identify one scanner that met the resolution requirement on campus at the School of Electric Computer Engineering. However, due to the challenge of scanning the inside of a soft leather hat, we were not able to create a complete look of the inside. The challenge was how to handle scanning complex textures and managing surface variations of the artifacts. Dark or shiny objects proved to be particularly time-consuming and problematic. In some cases, objects can be greased with a developer spray that prepares the surface and creates an ideal environment for scanning, thus decreasing distortion. However, when it comes to working with rare or delicate artifacts such as items in the archives, these solutions are not an option. With unexpected issues like this, the instructors want to make sure the project plan is drafted as detailed as possible to help students accurately budget time and plan alternative solutions if necessary. Specifically for this project, the students had to modify the design to incorporate the hat without interactive function.

At the end of the project cycle, it is also critical to consider archiving and preservation solutions for these projects. This step is important for both preserving the scholarship of the VR research section and providing examples and inspiration for future students and the general VR community. When it comes to preservation, there is a lack of mature solutions of

VR/3D content preservation for academic purposes. As Lischer-Katz and Cook made clear in their research: "Studies on the preservation and curation of 3D/VR have pointed out that as researchers increasingly use these technologies, there will be a greater need for archiving and preservation services. As emerging technologies, however, there is still a lack of knowledge about how best to create and curate the scholarly products of 3D/VR projects" (2019). Preserving and showcasing AR/VR/MR projects is a current challenge facing academic libraries and the whole of academia.

This project, along with others, repeated the implementation theme: expect unexpected setbacks and be flexible about making changes. Coming out of the class, what the instructors hope to install in these sessions are that students experiment with VR technologies, see how tools and platforms work, run into issues, and learn from the troubleshooting process. At a higher level, also guide students through a research process and mentor their information collection and analysis, decision-making and revising, and time management toward completing these projects. To optimize the learning experience, the instructors emphasize creating a "learn from your mistake" culture. At the end of each semester, project teams need to submit a project report to include their design, resources, implementation, and challenges they encountered in the process.

Assessment Tools

Assessment is an integral part of instruction and service development. It is essential at the beginning of a class or service to assure the alignment of objectives and intended outcomes, and to incorporate students' feedback. Assessment opportunities channel into the positive process-oriented practices that students can enact.

Rubrics

Rubrics are a tool to assess student work. The document lists concrete elements that the students or their projects will exhibit during the project and identify levels of success or engagement with each element. Some potential categories include technical skills and craftsmanship, communication of ideas, usability, student reflection, group engagement, problem-solving, or experimentation. The items you choose to include in the rubric will demonstrate to the student what the important learning objectives are. The levels of success can include (1) mastery or exceptional, (2) exceeding expectations, (3) meeting expectations, (4) needing improvement, and (5) incomplete.

- *Technical skills & craftsmanship* refer to the skills students would be employing to physically create their AR or VR products. These skills might include using the hardware or software properly, effectively modeling their subjects, editing, sound recording, unity of color palettes, and other skills. Decide a baseline skill level that you would like all projects to "meet expectations," especially with skills that are covered in the initial refresher lessons. This baseline allows for students to pass by meeting the objectives and leaves room for exceptional work as well.
- *Communication of ideas* refers to the ease with which users can understand the concepts in the project that the creators wished to convey. When assessing this point, review the student's statement of purpose and the project prompt to see what concepts are important to the creator or team. Then compare the intended concepts to the information conveyed through the composition of the AR or VR project (imagery, sound, sequence, movements, and so on) to see how closely the actual project relates to the ideas. This topic may also consider elements and principles of design, design hierarchy, and general legibility.
- *Usability* refers to how easily users can engage with the project. This topic might include how teams arrange menus, how the environment directs the viewer's attention, how easily viewers can navigate the virtual environment, and how seamlessly motions or interaction points are indicated. On the rubric itself, this item might include a list of markers for user engagement that teams can use as a checklist when making design decisions.
- *Reflection* is a key component of creative work. As described in the next section, student reflections are places for students to consider what they have learned and created. The students may reflect on the ideas they worked with, the process of creation, and the outcomes of the final project. The reflection rubric can look for evidence of complex thought, project planning, problem-solving skills, identification of skills learned, identification of what elements of the project are working and which parts need further improvement.
- *Group engagement* refers to individual contributions and teamwork within a group and during class activities or discussion. This item

ought not to penalize introverts for fewer public displays of enthusiasm compared to extroverts. Some contributions may be more subtle than others. This rubric element can also take into account feedback from other team members as well.

- *Problem-solving* refers to a student's willingness to ask questions, identify problems, and solve challenges as they arose during the project process.
- *Experimentation* is a useful segment to consider if the project might include difficult, complicated, or "stretch goal" aspects. This category encourages students to focus more on the process than on the final project. It can also reward students for creative risk-taking (which might not always work in the end or within the given time limits) and for iterating and editing a project during the creation period.

Student Reflections

Student reflections are an opportunity for them to consider what they have created and why in order to integrate it into their educational story. The reflections are an opportunity to express themselves in a variety of ways through the use of multimedia technologies. For example, reflections can take the form of written documents, video recordings, or audio podcasts or narrations. In any case, the reflections should encourage self-examination of both the final project and of the process of creating it. Reflection is a key aspect of the creative life of artists/creators, and it helps students of all ages grow as learners. Students often benefit from having a series of prompts to guide them through the reflection process.

Critiques

Critiques are informal or formal sharing and discussion periods that help students clarify their work and provide a structured time for peer and instructor feedback. Critiques can be very useful if they are held at multiple points in the design process. For example, a critique in the middle of a project can be used to streamline imagery or edit a mock-up, while one near the end can be used to troubleshoot the existing interactive design (similar to "user testing" or "beta testing"). It's valuable to emphasize that participants seek constructive criticism with specific detail (e.g., design legibility, use of composition or the elements of art and principles of design, and points of viewer engagement). During these reviews, students also get to see each other's work and identify the ways that peers have solved similar design challenges to their own. Seeing one's own work with new eyes, or through a peer's perspective, can provide new ideas or new readings that the original creator might not have considered!

Exhibition or Open Lab

Exhibitions or special invitations to the community to visit the VR Lab can be an excellent formal ending to a long project. It also makes a very concrete deadline! These exhibitions have multiple benefits to the curriculum. They provide external incentives or motivation for students to do their best work since they will be sharing it with a wider group of people. The exhibition lets other people in the community see what you and your students are working on. It can also be a chance to show what organizations or which professionals are partnering with the library/institution. Similarly, it provides a chance for your program to develop public interest and community engagement by letting people know about what your students are learning. Students can share their projects with friends, family, and other classmates.

An exhibition or open lab also provides real-world experience in planning and executing an event. Depending on age level, students can be engaged in many aspects of the event: choosing where the exhibition will be, writing a proposal for the space, dividing up tasks for how they will show the final projects, creating ads and flyers, installing the projects or workstations, adding informational tags and displaying student statements or reflections, and finally being present at the event to welcome and talk to visitors! Students may also wish to create informational posters that can be displayed near the demonstration areas. These posters can describe the project's intent, details about the class, faculty or guest contributors, and otherwise give context to the visitors. Finally, the exhibition or open lab can be a great résumé item for students.

Standards

Many different standards-issuing bodies exist. Some that might be useful to your lessons, depending on institution and student age ranges, appear in the following list. Review each framework to see which type best matches the content you are covering in your project. Reflective writing exercises and community engagement can help your class meet applicable standards, as well.

- American Association of School Libraries Standards for Learners and Librarians (AASL): https://standards.aasl.org/framework/
- C3 Social Studies Standards (C3): https://www.socialstudies.org/standards/c3
- Common Core State Standards (CCSS): and state-specific aligned standards http://www.corestandards.org/
- International Society for Technology in Education Standards for Students (ISTE): https://www.iste.org/standards/iste-standards-for-students
- National Core Art Standards Anchor Standards (NCAS): https://www.nationalartsstandards.org/
- Next Generation Science Standards (NGSS): https://www.nextgenscience.org/ The NGSS Topic of Engineering, Technology, and Applications of Science at the High School level is most applicable to these sample VR projects.

Here are two projects and possible standards that could be associated with the project. The examples will focus primarily on high school–level standards (grades 9–12) when applicable. Depending on your class, you will need to customize your selected standards by subject and grade level.

Use Case #1: Virtual Tour of Campus

Referencing the virtual campus tour we described earlier in the chapter, some of the major skills that are expected of students in a project of this nature include:

- Information collection
- Information analysis and quality
- Decision-making
    - What information or visual elements to include in the project
    - Prioritizing information
    - Conveying information to viewer/user

- Revising and flexibility
  - Alternative solutions
- Time management
- Report writing and analysis (implementation and challenges)
- Technological tool use
  - Building or creating
  - Recording
  - Formatting
  - Exporting
- Technology troubleshooting
- Technology experimentation and iteration
- Presentation of project to peers and community
- User communication, navigation, interaction

Some applicable standards for the standards frameworks listed include:

- AASL: On this form, each standard domain contains four subskill competencies that individuals might be using (think, create, share, and grow). Find the complete standards at this link: https://standards.aasl.org/wp-content/uploads/2018/08/180206-AASL-framework-for-learners-2.pdf
- C3: Find detailed information about the standards at this link: https://www.socialstudies.org/system/files/2022/c3-framework-for-social-studies-rev0617.2.pdf
  - Dimension 1, "Developing Questions & Planning Inquiries"
  - Dimension 3, "Evaluating Sources & Using Evidence"
- CCSS: Anchor Standards for Writing for College and Career Readiness. Find the standards at http://www.corestandards.org
  - CCSS.ELA-LITERACY.CCRA.W.2
  - CCSS.ELA-LITERACY.CCRA.W.4
  - CCSS.ELA-LITERACY.CCRA.W.6
  - CCSS.ELA-LITERACY.CCRA.W.10
- ISTE: Note that each standard contains four specific subskills that students might be using. Detailed descriptions of each student standard can

be found at this link: https://www.iste.org/standards/iste-standards-for-students

- NCAS, Media Arts: Note that each anchor standard includes multiple examples of the standard put into practice for different grade levels pre–K through high school. The Media Arts standards can be found in PDF form at https://www.nationalartsstandards.org/sites/default/files/Media%20Arts%20at%20a%20Glance%20-%20new%20copyright%20info.pdf

Use Case #2: Immersive Galapagos Island Environment

This project, mentioned in Chapter 2, took place in a short-term ten-day school trip. High school students combined skills in biology, visual arts, and computer science to record animal and plant life in the Galapagos Islands. On return to campus after the trip, students created an immersive mural with access points to view augmented reality recordings and 360-degree video from the islands. Some of the major skills that are expected of students in this project include:

- Information collection and analysis
- Decision-making
  - Selecting information
  - Prioritizing information
  - Conveying information to viewer/user
- Team collaboration and communication
- Time management
- Technological tool use
  - Building models
  - Recording audio and video
  - Formatting files
  - Exporting media and files
- Technology troubleshooting
- Technology experimentation and iteration
- User communication: navigation, interaction within virtual environment
- Presentation of project to peers and community

Some applicable standards for the standards frameworks listed include:

- AASL: Note that each standard domain contains four subskill competencies that individuals might be using (think, create, share, and grow). Find the complete standards at this link: https://standards.aasl.org/wp-content/uploads/2018/08/180206-AASL-framework-for-learners-2.pdf
- C3: Find detailed information about the standards at this link: https://www.socialstudies.org/system/files/2022/c3-framework-for-social-studies-rev0617.2.pdf in PDF form
    - Dimension 1, "Developing Questions & Planning Inquiries"
    - Dimension 3, "Evaluating Sources & Using Evidence"
    - CCSS Anchor Standards for Writing for College and Career Readiness
    - CCSS.ELA-LITERACY.CCRA.W.2
    - CCSS.ELA-LITERACY.CCRA.W.4
    - CCSS.ELA-LITERACY.CCRA.W.6
- ISTE: Note that each standard contains four specific subskills that students might be using. Detailed descriptions for each student standard can be found at this link: https://www.iste.org/standards/iste-standards-for-students
- NCAS, Media Arts: Note that each anchor standard includes multiple examples of the standard put into practice for different grade levels pre–K through high school. The Media Arts standards can be found in PDF form at https://www.nationalartsstandards.org/sites/default/files/Media%20Arts%20at%20a%20Glance%20-%20new%20copyright%20info.pdf

REFERENCES

ACRL. 2015. "Framework for information literacy for higher education." American Library Association. February 9. http://www.ala.org/acrl/standards/ilframework.

Cai, Zhihui, Peipei Mao, Dandan Wang, Jinbo He, Xinjie Chen, and Xitao Fan. 2022. "Effects of scaffolding in digital game-based learning on student's achievement: A three-level meta-analysis." *Educational Psychology Review* 34 (2): 537–574.

Chang, Yunjeong, and Peggy Brickman. 2018. "When group work doesn't work: Insights from students." *CBE—Life Sciences Education* 17 (ar52) (Fall): 1–17. https://www.lifescied.org/doi/epdf/10.1187/cbe.17-09-0199.

Dumford, Amber D., and Angie L. Miller. 2018. "Online learning in higher education: Exploring advantages and disadvantages for engagement." *Journal of Computing in Higher Education* 30: 452–465. https://doi.org/10.1007/s12528-018-9179-z.

Hall, Nathan, Zack Lischer-Katz, Matt Cook, Juliet Hardesty, Jamie Wittenberg, Jennifer Johnson, Robert H. McDonald, and Tara Carlisle. "Supporting virtual reality and 3D in academic libraries: defining preservation and curation challenges." International Conference on Digital Preservation, 2019.

Hansen, Randall S. 2006. "Benefits and problems with student teams: Suggestions for improving team projects." *Journal of Education for Business* 82 (1): 11–19. doi: 10.3200/JOEB.82.1.11-19.

Houtman, Eveline. 2015. "'Mind-blowing': Fostering self-regulated learning in information literacy instruction." *Communications in Information Literacy* 9 (1): 6. https://pdxscholar.library.pdx.edu/comminfolit/vol9/iss1/6/.

Mackey, Thomas P., and Trudi E. Jacobson. 2011. "Reframing information literacy as a metaliteracy." *College & Research Libraries* 72 (1): 62–78. doi:10.5860/crl-76r1.

MacLeod, Miles, and Jan T. van der Veen. 2020. "Scaffolding interdisciplinary project-based learning: A case study." *European Journal of Engineering Education* 45 (3): 363–377. doi: 10.1080/03043797.2019.1646210.

McCarthy, Alma, and Thomas N. Garavan. 2008. "Team learning and metacognition: A neglected area of HRD research and practice." *Advances in Developing Human Resources* 10 (4): 509–524. doi:10.1177/1523422308320496.

Palincsar, Annemarie Sullivan. 1984. "Reciprocal Teaching: Working within the Zone of Proximal Development." Paper presented at the annual meeting of the American Educational Research Association, New Orleans, April. https://files.eric.ed.gov/fulltext/ED246385.pdf.

Robb, Meigan, and Teresa Shellenbarger. 2021. "The distracted online student: Strategies to capture attention and promote connection." *Teaching and Learning in Nursing* 16 (4): 389–392. https://doi.org/10.1016/j.teln.2021.05.008.

Schraw, Gregory. 1998. "Promoting general metacognitive awareness." *Instructional Science* 26 (1–2): 113–125. https://www.researchgate.net/publication/227166212_Promoting_General_Metacognitive_Awareness.

Simons, P. Robert-Jan. 2000. "Towards a constructivistic theory of self-directed learning." *Self-learning*: 1–12. https://dspace.library.uu.nl/bitstream/handle/1874/6994/5701.pdf?sequence=2

Unity Documentation. 2021. "Scenes." Unity User Manual 2021.3 (LTS). https://docs.unity3d.com/Manual/CreatingScenes.html.

Unity Manual. 2021. "Interactions." January 22, 2021. https://docs.unity3d.com/Packages/com.unity.inputsystem@1.0/manual/Interactions.html.

Wiltshire, Travis J., Kelly Rosch, Logan Fiorella, and Stephen M. Fiore. 2014. "Training for collaborative problem solving: Improving team process and performance through metacognitive prompting." *Proceedings of the Human Factors and Ergonomics Society Annual Meeting* 58 (1): 1154–1158. https://doi.org/10.1177/1541931214581241.

Zumbrunn, S., J. Tadlock, and E. Danielle Roberts. 2011. "Encouraging self-regulated learning in the classroom: A review of the literature." *Metropolitan Educational Research Consortium (MERC)*. https://www.researchgate.net/publication/325603134_Encouraging_self-regulated_learning_in_the_classroom_A_review_of_the_literature.

RESOURCES

Student Questionnaire Ideas

Examples of relevant topics to pursue with students include the following. See more questionnaire ideas in Chapter 2's Resources section.

- Previous experience with these technologies
- Relevant coding or 3D modeling experience
- General college major
- Research or personal interests
- Time constraints
- Available times for team meetings

Icebreaker Activities

Bingo

In this activity, the instructor creates bingo cards with descriptions for each square on the bingo card. Students connect with other students to find out who matches up with the descriptions on the cards. This gives the students a structured mechanism for discussion and an opportunity to get to know one another. Descriptions could include general topics such as favorite foods or traveling experiences. However, on the cards you could also include descriptions specific to activities that might be relevant to the class, such as preferred operating systems, experience with certain software, graphic artist, or photographer. This activity can be adapted for in person or online learning. Students can also submit description ideas ahead of time in their initial questionnaire. Instructors then gather those descriptions and later incorporate them into the bingo card.

Blank Bingo Card

		FREE SPACE		

Interview Pairs

Keeping things simple is always a good rule of thumb. For both online classes and in-person classes, having students chat with each other in pairs and then introduce the student they were paired with to the rest of the class is a simple yet effective way to promote peer interactions early in the process. Provide some structure for the activity such as four key questions to incorporate into the interview activity: (1) Name, pronouns, major, where they are from; (2) Hidden talents or sources of pride; (3) Interests; and (4) Objectives or goals in taking the class. This class can be adapted as an in-person activity that has students moving around the classroom or an online activity with breakout rooms.

Pair Interview Questions	
1. Name, pronouns, major, where they are from	2. Hidden talents or sources of pride
3. Interests or activities	4. Objectives or goals in taking this class

Best/Worst Class

Another activity that can both foster connections between students in a class and between students and their instructors is an activity that prompts students to share some of their best classes and worst classes. Students are asked to share what they consider to be one of their most positive class experiences, along with one that they didn't find enriching. Give them a few minutes to write their ideas down on paper, and then each person goes around and shares their educational memories. Students will likely relate to each other's negative and positive experiences, while instructors can use the activity to reflect on their own pedagogy.

What Do You Hope to Learn?

At the heart of most icebreaker activities is getting to know the personalities and interests of participants better. One of the main takeaways from an icebreaker in an educational setting is what an individual hopes to learn or gain through their participation. At the very least, an easy activity to get people talking to each other is the one thing everyone has in common; the class! Simply asking people what they hope to take away from their experience can shed light on personalities, interests, and ultimately will begin personal connections.

Peer Evaluation

Each student should evaluate every other student in the project.

Consider using a Likert 5 point scale:

- How often do you interact with this person?
  - (Scaled questions Not at all to Regularly)
- Did this person show initiative beyond assigned tasks?
  - (Scaled questions Not at all to Frequently)
  - If so, can you give one specific example (Free text short answer)
- Did this person mentor you or otherwise share critical knowledge with you that helped you on the project?
  - (Scaled Questions Strongly Disagree to Strongly Agree)
- Was this person engaged with subgroup activities? I.e., Showed up on time to meetings, was prompt in responding to communications.
  - (Scaled Questions Strongly Disagree to Strongly Agree)
- Did this team member provide their content and individual deliverables when promised?
  - (Scaled Questions Strongly Disagree to Strongly Agree)

Scaffolding Projects

Here are some sample questions to help get started as you support your students' project and personal learning goals.

- How can you help students break the project into manageable learning activities?
- What is the student's current skill level in the activities they will need for their project?
- What is the student's current course credit commitment?
- If applicable, do you and the student agree on the number of credits they should take for the class based on their personal learning goals?
- If the student's project is larger or has more intense coding or technological needs, how can you help them learn the basics of the technical tools they will need or help them find appropriate tutorial materials?

Project Team Roles

Note that these are suggestions and your student teams may not need to use all of these roles. They may also combine roles to better facilitate their particular project.

- **Coding and Programmer Role**
  - Coding skills in C++ or C#; these are especially useful when using Unity
  - Swift, JavaScript
  - Object-oriented programming concepts
  - SDK concepts
- **Media Creator, Camera Operator Role**
  - Filming and using a 360 camera
  - Volumetric capture-camera operators, green screen
- **3D Modeling Role: 3D Assets**
  - Knowledge of the asset store, use of pre-created assets
  - Modeling and texturing with Blender
  - Maya, Cinema4D
- **Audio Engineer Role: Music, Soundtracks**
  - Knowledge of audio production (microphones, mixers)
  - Audio editing in Adobe Audition or Audacity
- **Graphic Designer, Technical Artist Role**
  - Mockups
  - Graphic creation in the Adobe Creative Suite
- **Scripting, Storyboarding, Writer Role**
- **Researcher Role**

Project Structure Elements

- Key areas to structure time for include:
  - Play—time for students to learn what aspects, tools, or team roles they are more interested in
  - Practice—"Sandbox" practice site where students can learn and develop skills on a smaller scale or a less intense project
  - Formal work time

- Playtesting or beta testing
- Growth and iteration
- Reflection
- Presentation
- Archiving

Storyboarding Diagram

Storyboarding is a strategy for sketching out the different scenes that will occur in the student's virtual environment. The storyboard rectangles can capture the basic shape or composition for each scene or state that the viewer can encounter. While the viewer may not pass through the scenes in a linear sequence, the diagram can help students plan what they will be designing during the project, including any transition scenes.

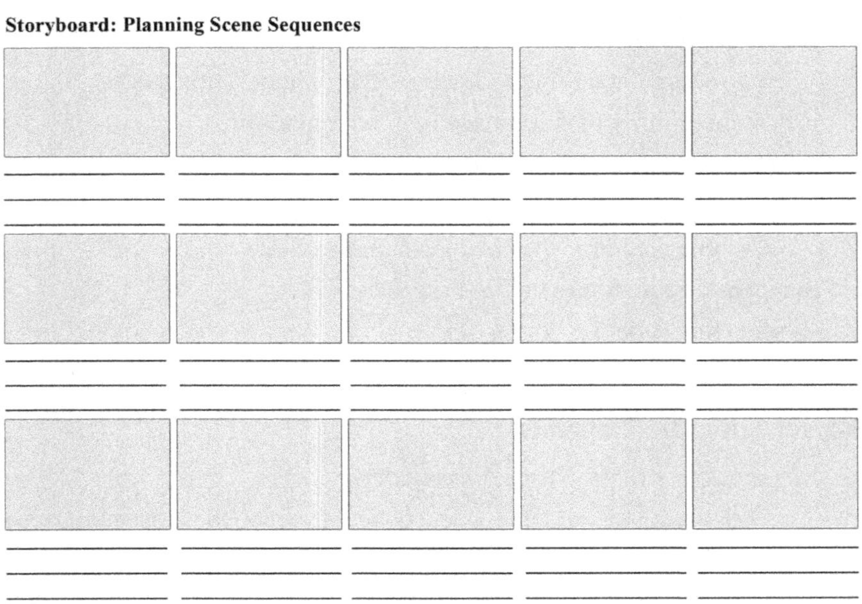

Figure 4-2 Example of a storyboard format to use for planning scene sequences

Scene-Planning Diagram

The scene-planning diagram takes each scene or setting from the storyboarding diagram and further develops the contents of it. In the small rectangles, the student can sketch variations on the arrangement, orientation, or composition of the scene. Once the student has a favorite, the student can sketch the scene with more detail in the larger rectangle at the bottom left. The right column provides space for students to map out what kind of content they will need to create (or find) for this particular scene, ideas for where they can find these resources, and specific identification of sites where the viewer/user will interact with items in the scene.

Scene Planning **Project:** ________________

Practice Sketches of Scene

Sketch of Scene

Content (circle):
Still or 360-degree images?
Video Recording?
Audio Recoring?
3D Scans?
3D Models?
Environment Model?

Resources:

Sites for Viewer Interaction:

Figure 4-3 Example of a scene-planning format to use for developing project goals and milestones

Semester-Long Project Guide (15–17 Weeks)

- Week 1–3: Introduction to curriculum, classmates, and software
- Week 4: Project teams assigned and begin design planning
- Week 5: Project teams pitch designs for implementation on VR devices

- Week 6–8: Teams build first draft of project
- Week 9/Midterms: Practice, troubleshoot, and playtest internally with feedback
- Week 10–12: Teams continue to build project. Iteration and instructor support
- Week 13–15: Continued building, iteration, and instructor support
- Week 16–17: Community playtest event and feedback

Semester Guide with Multiple Projects (15–17 Weeks)

- Week 1–3: Introduction to curriculum, classmates, and software
- Week 4: First small project to show proficiency with software
- Week 5: Second small project to build on skills learned in first project
- Week 6–7: Longer third project that continues to build on skills
- Week 8/Midterms: Presentation, playtesting, internal class feedback on third project
- Week 9: Project teams assigned and begin design planning for final project
- Week 10–12: Project teams pitch designs for implementation on VR devices
- Week 13–15: Teams build final project. Iteration and instructor support
- Week 16–17: Community playtest event and feedback for final project

Template for a Lesson Plan

- Lesson Plan Title

  ____

  ____

  ____

  ____

  ____

- Overview or Purpose

- Essential Question

- Education Standards

- Tools, Equipment, and Materials Needed

- Verification to Check for Student Understanding

- Steps for the Actual Activity

____

____

____

____

____

____

____

- Assessment, Reflection, and Exhibitions

____

____

____

____

____

____

____

Rubric Components

- The levels of student success can include (1) mastery or exceptional, (2) exceeding expectations, (3) meeting expectations, (4) needing improvement, and (5) incomplete.
- Possible Rubric Elements
    - Technical skills
    - Craftsmanship
    - Communication of ideas
    - Usability
    - Reflection
    - Group engagement (see peer evaluation questionnaire)
    - Problem-solving
    - Experimentation and creative risks

A Simple Rubric

Table 4-1

Student Level	Exceptional	Exceeding Expectations	Meeting Expectations	Needing Improvement	Incomplete
Skill Category	**4**	**3**	**2**	**1**	**0**
Technical Skills	Deft and seamless use of technology	Efficient use of skills	Apt use of workable skills	Skills are developing but not proficient	Not evident
Communication of Ideas	Insightful and confident communication	Effectively communicate concepts and actions	Generally clear communication to the user	Communication is confusing in places	Unintelligible
Usability	Polished and professional, intuitive usability	Straightforward, easily operated	Usable and manageable	Clunky and difficult to use at times	Difficult to use or understand

Student Reflection Questions

- What was the project prompt, and how does your project address the prompt?
- What are your initial or evolving goals for the project?
- How did you and your teammates divide up the aspects of the project into manageable tasks?
- What was the most successful part of the project?
- What was the most complicated, challenging, or unexpected part of the project?
- Did your project change over the course of the class or as a result of user feedback?
- What parts of the project still need improvement?
- What are one or two major skills you developed during this project?
- What did you most enjoy about the project?
- If this project was offered in a future class, what changes would you suggest to make the project a better experience for students?
- Did you have an "ah-ha" moment during the project? If so, describe what you discovered or realized.

Questions for Users to Answer during Critiques

- What parts felt most effective?
- What was the coolest or most engaging part?
- What parts felt confusing?
- Where would you like more guidance?

Exhibition or Open Lab Preparation Questions

- Where will the event take place?
- When will the event take place? How long will the event be?
- What materials need to be set up ahead of time? How will the tasks be assigned?
- Who will make sure the technological elements are charged, prepared, and accessible?

- What labels or posters are necessary to help your users orient themselves or better understand the projects? Who will create them?
- Will students be present at the event to explain their projects and answer questions? How will you divide up the shifts?
- Who will be invited to the event?
  - Will you need to make any special accommodations for them to access your institution?
  - Will you need to put up signs or directions or provide a map of your event location?
- How will you or the students promote the event?

FIVE

Sustaining Community through Peer Learning and Partnerships

This chapter will cover strategies to maintain program momentum beyond the bounds of the classroom. As elaborated on in the previous chapter, building community and encouraging student engagement are ways to keep your program active and growing. In a typical classroom environment, the sense of community that organically forms through shared learning experiences can end when the class ends. However, libraries with a designated AR/VR/MR service space or specialized labs that are permanent in nature have the unique ability to retain and continue the sense of community and learning beyond the semester or beyond the project time frame.

COMMUNITY IN EDUCATION

An active community of practice is critical to students' learning experiences outside of the classroom. To encourage these kinds of communities in libraries, one promising model is pairing technology-oriented service points in libraries with a strong instructional program that engages students and complements the day-to-day services the library offers. Within this model, the core community members are students who participate in the instructional program. Over time, they build a connection with dedicated library employees and other enthusiasts who work with emerging technologies. The skills acquired from the instructional program prepare students for more in-depth self-guided learning. As student skill sets expand, they can share their knowledge with other community members. Over time, this community will grow and will likely have members of varying skill levels. Newer members can learn from more experienced developers and contribute to the collective knowledge base. This framework dissolves the typical barriers of a standard classroom experience and creates a more sustainable and impactful educational environment.

To encourage the community aspect of learning, librarians should explore the potential of developing programs that go beyond drop-in workshops, and instead, move toward integrating educational programming in which libraries build stronger connections with students. Educational programming that fosters community would allow students to spend more time with librarians; this might take the form of classes more akin to a certificate series, ongoing research, or college credit. Libraries lend themselves to not only self-driven learning but also project-based learning (PBL) that builds community. Project-based learning is described as an approach in which students actively explore real-world problems and challenges while engaging in personally meaningful projects (PBLWorks, n.d.). Prohl states, "Project-based learning provides the students with the best chance for academic success and generates positive community involvement." He goes on to say PBL "provides a framework for a curriculum shift from stand-alone classes focused solely on content knowledge to content-enriched learning experiences" (2022). What can we as library educators do to encourage content-enriched learning experiences that foster community? A study done by Kinberg discovered that student learning improved when the educational setting changed (2020). The idea is that we could create a more authentic learning experience for the student by going outside of a traditional classroom location setting. Prohl notes, "Growing and adapting educational settings continue to promote student engagement alongside community relations. Bringing into the mix the community at large is crucial to the students' success. From public libraries to nature centers, community relations are vital" (2022). Libraries can leverage their natural position and role as community center, academic facilitator, or campus connector to reimagine the educational setting and continually adapt to support these efforts. For example, a location setting change could take the form of students and librarians partnering on research in a library archive, students and librarians developing a virtual or Web-based exhibit to showcase library resources, or a library developing programs that put students in direct contact with researchers, scholars, industry experts, or artists to collaborate on joint ventures. When the library reimagines its role to go beyond solely that of information repository to one that encompasses the role of active community research participant, educational partner, and project manager, this sets the stage for a diverse, inclusive, and community-driven educational experience for students.

Higher-Ed Case Study: AR/VR/MR Community at Georgia Tech Library

The VR research class we have been using as an example throughout this book is part of the Georgia Tech Library's growing effort to not only expand instructional programming but support VR research and development on campus. In addition to this class, the library also operates a virtual reality service point available to the entire campus. The service point provides students with access to headsets and appropriate software and hardware for the development environment. This service was originally piloted in the Data Visualization lab with no dedicated staff. In order to maximize the use and engagement with these specialized resources, team members collaborated on teaching, research support, and equipment management. The librarians who began the project felt it was important to start small, gauge community interest, and then scale appropriately. With growing interest in the library's VR research class, a few students stayed on and worked collaboratively with librarians to mentor future students. In doing so, these students built up their own skill set and became advanced developers, in addition to encouraging their peers. The class also spawned some game nights, meetup groups, and discussions with researchers on campus about emerging topics in the field. It is hoped that over time this community will continue to grow including students, researchers, industry experts, and general enthusiasts, all who can contribute to the collective knowledge. In this type of environment, people learn from each other rather than from the librarians only.

Students from the library research class are the early members and mentors of this community. Since these classes are small groups of four to eight students per semester, the instructors were able to establish strong bonds with each one of them through targeted involvement with their project process, from project design and minor adjustments to resource needs, technical hurdles and solutions, as well as dealing with the stress and frustration they might encounter while working on a set of new technical tools. This experience builds a connection beyond the class. Many students expressed their positive learning experience during the end-of-semester reflections. Library instructors were able to support these students beyond the class by encouraging them to showcase their research to potential employers and providing references when appropriate. Additionally, the class exposed them to hands-on coding and important resources available to them on campus and online. With the strong connection to the library built through their investment and interest in VR research, many of the students, if on campus, stay connected to the librarians and fellow students year after year. These same students offered to share their experiences and assist VR researchers on campus with troubleshooting. Their work with the library put them in direct contact with other AR/VR communities of practice on campus.

Additional important members of this community are the researchers on campus. As AR/VR/MR use has grown, there have been labs across disciplines at Georgia Tech using it for their research, including but not limited to engineering, psychology, humanity, and various technical training centers. Over years of collaboration, the library has built connections with the College of Liberal Arts for research and College of Engineering on a device-sharing program, as well as other campus offices in this domain. For instance, psychology research groups utilized the library lab space to test some of their projects. These campus partnerships contribute to the sense of community for AR/VR at Georgia Tech.

A third group within this community are simply VR enthusiasts. These are people interested in emerging technologies primarily through playing games, but they may not have done significant development projects with devices. In some cases, these enthusiasts will become developers when their community experience is a positive one, and they are able to learn from their peers and actively engage with others who share similar interests.

To create an open and welcoming culture, the technology-oriented service points at the Georgia Tech Library invite users with different levels of experience to participate and will recommend resources based on their knowledge and interests. Experienced community members have been an enormous help to beginning-level members in the past by joining them on project design discussions and hands-on troubleshooting sessions.

Before COVID, the library hosted VR Interest Group meetups, during which we invited VR researchers from the metro Atlanta area to come in and talk about their projects. One example project of inspiration is Open World Atlanta (Georgia State University, n.d.). In the future, more AR/VR/MR developers from outside the metro area will be considered and approached to participate in project presentations and panels. It is hoped that these activities will serve to inspire future students who participate in the VR research class and continue the tradition of sustained and ongoing communities of practice.

K–12 Case Study: VR Community at Mount Vernon

The Virtual Reality Lab at Mount Vernon was built around the central question, "What if high school students were given the opportunity to work with leaders in the technology industry, not on school projects, but on projects that have authentic impact and intersect many industries?" (Mount Vernon School 2017). All of the connections with the lab grow from students and faculty reaching out to the community on campus and inviting them to partner with the VR Lab.

The VR Lab has hosted lower and upper school students for creative academic endeavors. In the fall of 2019, VR students created 3D paintings with the *Tiltbrush* program. The VR students collaborated with Music & Film students to create and record compositions that paired with each 3D painting. After the completion of the project, the "virtual reality class hosted a Virtual Art Museum for their peers and teachers" to have an immersive virtual art journey in the upper (Neylon 2019). VR students do not have to build all of the environments experienced at the school. Later that year, 2019, upper school anatomy students virtually transported themselves into "the musculoskeletal system" during a visit to the VR lab (Houston 2019). Partnerships like this, with classes in other departments, can include third-party virtual reality programs tailored to the visiting class's particular subject area. Note that it's usually a good idea to review the VR content yourself before sharing with learners, especially when working with younger students. During the lower school's "Spring Expeditions," students in the first 1st grade partnered with upper school juniors to try on "Oculus googles for a personalized walk on the moon" (Mount Vernon School 2022).

Through these activities, MR students not only built an enthusiastic VR researcher and user community, they also applied these skills in the real world to facilitate learning and content creation.

BUILDING COMMUNITY

We have emphasized the importance of maintaining community beyond the class or project parameters. As we consider pairing library services with research efforts, it is important to link these activities to a mechanism that will facilitate community building. By doing so, librarians can integrate an element of play or social activity with the research that will encourage further engagement and interest. Having community engagement in mind and including that component along with your research initiatives creates a natural channel for communication and connection outside of the formal academic environment. In Table 5-1, we outline a few sample library service points, how those service points might be linked to research, and finally how a library might facilitate community involvement and encourage topical discussions.

Table 5-1

Library Service Point	Associated Research/Project	Mechanism for Building Community
Device and periphery lending service point	Students are researching how 360 cameras are used.	Host a photography-themed event that invites students to document a meaningful place with cameras. Consider an exhibit of the work produced and provide opportunities for photographers to meet with each other in library spaces to discuss their work.
Media labs	Students are researching uses for advanced graphics and modeling software.	Invite students and community members to a speaking engagement from an industry professional who specializes in using graphic design software or 3D modeling. Have the speaker share how they got their start. Local industries are often eager to connect with neighboring universities or schools.
Data visualization services	Students are working with large data sets and researching the most effective ways to share this information.	If an in-person event is too costly or not possible, facilitate a virtual speaking event or webinar on zoom or similar platform. Invite a scientist who is disseminating their research to a broad audience to come and present techniques for

Table 5-1 (*Continued*)

Library Service Point	Associated Research/Project	Mechanism for Building Community
		creating effective visualizations. Create follow-up activities after the webinar concludes. Consider creating a series; the repetitive nature of ongoing extracurricular events will assist in forming community.
Audio or video recording studios	Students are researching the importance of oral histories.	Host a lunch-and-learn where students discover more about audio recording and production techniques. Or another example might be to host a sound walk. Participants can use simple recording devices to record the natural sounds of their environment. Facilitate listening activities after the walk that give participants the opportunity to share experiences and converse.
VR Lab	Students are researching the use of virtual reality for teaching and learning.	The library hosts a VR game night to introduce immersive environments to those who may not have experienced one. The game night becomes a monthly event that could draw in some of the same people.

ENGAGING COMMUNITY, NONTRADITIONAL EDUCATORS, AND VISITING ARTISTS

The interaction between librarians and nontraditional teachers, including visual artists, during programming adds value to the educational partnership. Depending on the individuals involved, the instructors might bring technical skills, compositional skills, administrative skills, funding information, or historical and content-related knowledge. A nontraditional teacher might lead discussions in unexpected directions to inspire creative sparks.

The visual arts can be a valuable tool for learning and processing information. Visiting artists add the creative process and methods of artistic communication to the learning experience. First, hands-on projects give students the opportunity to ask, "what would work if . . .?" as they actively process and communicate their knowledge. Second, students have to concisely convey their concepts visually. This conciseness requires students to research and understand their subject before translating the concepts into a visual medium that must also clearly communicate to the users. The user's experience of the content defines the success of the project, so students must create clear, interesting, and distinct environments and interactions that the users can easily navigate. Third, observation is a key aspect of visual arts as well as some nonart disciplines. One UPenn Study (Penn Medicine 2017) states that ophthalmologist students improved their ability to observe and describe diagnoses after taking an art observation course at the Philadelphia Museum of Art. Fourth, it's important to acknowledge that a student doesn't have to be a visual artist to contribute to the creative process. This process uses many of the "21st Century Learning" This process uses skills such as collaboration, critical thinking, creativity, communication, and confidence. In a 2013 study, Google's top characteristics of success were: "being a good coach, communicating and listening well, possessing insights into others' values and points of view, having empathy and being supportive of colleagues, being a good critical thinker and problem solver, and being able to make connections across complex ideas" (Strauss 2017).

These are all broad, foundational skills that an arts-related project can practice. Through the integration of arts projects into nonart disciplines, students can develop tools to practice being more connective, creative, and explorative people. Visual artists can bring in the useful reflection of critiques, which is a common part of visual art education. A "critique" is an active process for sharing and discussing creative work. It is useful to foster a supportive and constructive critique setting in the classroom where students, instructors, and guest educators can thoughtfully discuss what aspects of a project are working, what design choices were made (intentionally or unintentionally), places that get confusing, and what needs improvement.

As mentioned in the previous chapter, a complicated emerging technology project has many different roles for students to take on. Consider the different roles your students are playing, and invite professionals in your community to consult with the project teams. These nontraditional educators can offer students advice, help them streamline their project, suggest improvements, or give reassurance. Note that with the improved ubiquity of videoconferencing, your guest professionals might not be physically present in your classroom!

COMMUNITY AND PROJECT-BASED LEARNING

Project-based learning thrives in community environments, and in return, helps grow and sustain the community. Under this learning model, different research tracks give students opportunities to further explore the resources, knowledge, and information of specific project steps. Peer support and collaboration brings the team together to educate each other on their learnings and assemble individual components to a complete project. The process of exploring, learning, and solving problems together builds strong bonds among students in class and beyond.

Project-based learning also creates opportunities for students to connect to their peers outside the class. While working on these projects, student researchers can invite their peers to be test users throughout phases of their projects. Test users, preferably with different levels of familiarity with innovative immersive technology, can provide valuable feedback to the creator-students for improvement. User experience testing and the gathering of feedback are one way to build community around each project in and outside of the class.

The presentation portion of the project cycle also presents opportunities for connecting to new students and potentially draw them into the program. That is, inviting new students to the final presentations is a fun and inspiring way to show them the possibilities of these immersive technologies. These new students might not have considered joining a VR class before experiencing the technology in person. Some of the project presentations could also be used as outreach materials on campus at tabling events, club presentations, and for curriculum advisors/mentors. Beyond the campus community, selected students' projects could be presented at new or prospective student orientations as a channel to reach a broader range of potential students.

Another channel for community learning is through the sharing of documentation. While students are working on their projects, they should be given clear instruction about documenting new resources found, challenges encountered and solutions proposed, if any solution is working and why, and other important troubleshooting sessions and lessons learnt. This information is going to be passed along to the next class. Besides project documentation, instructors can also maintain a record of "best practices" to help the next class of students, drawing on information gleaned in the end-of-project reports. Best practices include identifying what are the most helpful things that the students learned each time. Keeping this record accessible and searchable can help reduce mistakes and hurdles for students and instructors alike. This record can also be a tool to share with new cross-curricular partners, community partners, or new instructors as you set up your best practices and class norms with the new incoming students and colleagues. These documentations over time create a knowledge base for students' learning and class improvement.

COMMUNITY AND PARTNERSHIP

As interests grow in these emerging technologies for research and learning, campus collaborations will become more active than ever before. Funding sources are not always readily available regardless of whether you are in a college environment or K–12. Thus, to keep up with the research needs, it is advisable to develop partnerships with campus and external stakeholders.

The unique advantage of the library is its openness to the whole campus regardless of discipline or grade level. At the center of people and ideas, libraries offer a hub of space and resources to students, faculty, and staff across the campus. As a result, the library attracts partners who want to promote their devices, test their projects, and connect with other campus units. Depending on the nature and structure of an organization, there may be other units on campus with hardware, development officers, or access to specialized resources that are willing to share them or related information. Collecting and updating such information is an iterative process.

As important as hardware and skills are, ideas fuel the creative energy of library services. A growing program focusing on technologies should become a hub of research ideas. Again, depending on the organization, these ideas could be more research-focused such as collaborations with an academic unit, or practice-driven such as collaborations with an administrative department. Coming with these ideas are other opportunities for the community, such as chances for student developers to solve real-world

See the resources at the end of the chapter for a list of starter questions for getting to know peer organizations.

problems and have their names associated with these projects, sometimes funding opportunities, and potential collaborative programming such as a hackathon. By pulling these project ideas in, libraries really close the loop of collecting resources, training skills, fueling ideas, creating prototypes or products with research or practical value, and carving a professional path in the process for students involved.

Higher-Ed Case Study: Collaboration with Campus Partners at Georgia Tech

One collaboration Georgia Tech Library was able to form is a device-sharing program with the College of Engineering. The College of Engineering was able to secure funds for new devices including HoloLens and Magic Leap. With the new devices they were trying to explore students' research potential. With the library recognized as an interdisciplinary service point on campus as well as an open space for VR development, they offered to share one of their HoloLens with the library's device lending program so that the headsets were more accessible to campus users. As of fall 2022, the library is going through this pilot phase to test user interests while exploring this new service model and partnership.

If this program is successful, we will consider expanding the collaboration with more device sharing and potentially a campus AR/VR/MR hackathon hosted in the library.

Another important collaborator on campus is the Center for 21st Century Universities (hereafter the center), which is a research branch of the provost office to innovate education (Georgia Institute of Technology, n.d.). The center reaches out to seek more development opportunities that expand research on campus. The library has been participating in the conversation to help polish project ideas, contribute to institute research, and is acting as a key connector for stakeholders on campus. As a central hub of people, devices and ideas on AR/VR/MR, we see ourselves connecting all parties of interests and distributing skills and ideas on campus.

As collaboration grows, it can be beneficial to have a system to manage all efforts and resources. For example, at the Georgia Tech Library, service points organize our collaboration and resource distribution with partners external to the library through written service-level agreements, which clarifies the scope of work, such as IT support, device loaning, space use, and financial responsibilities among other responsibilities.

With limited resources to expand services, especially the resource-demanding ones like AR/VR services, collaboration is key to success. Through these collaborative programs, we have been able to collectively offer our resources and information in support of research and learning.

K–12 Case Study: Collaboration with External Partners at Mount Vernon

The Virtual Reality Lab at Mount Vernon School takes many opportunities to connect with the community on campus, in the greater Atlanta area, and with companies across the world.

Mount Vernon VR students have partnered with organizations in the Atlanta community. The VR club worked with Children's Healthcare of Atlanta (CHOA) "to create a VR program to help patients who are going through physical therapy," with the idea that greater patient comfort will allow the treatment to be more effective (Mount Vernon School 2020). The students led the research, creating "over 75 questions" that they used "to interview both the medical professionals and the patients themselves" (Graham 2019). The final program, the Island, "serves as a distraction from pain and encourages patients to use their bodies better during physical therapy sessions by bending, stretching, squatting and moving throughout the virtual island" (Mount Vernon School 2020). In 2018, a small team of students created an exhibit for the Center for Civil and Human Rights open to the public throughout the summer (Mount Vernon School 2018b). The immersive experience included rally footage and interviews. The students wanted to emphasize how much "virtual reality is a fantastic medium for storytelling" (Mount Vernon School 2018b).

Corporate partnerships have helped the educational team build out the VR Lab. In 2018, the school partnered with Dell/Alienware to set up VR headsets and computer workstations. One of the instructors had connected with Dell/Alienware representatives on LinkedIn, sharing "the students' vision for a powerful partnership . . . where students can conduct real-time VR research and create engaging VR content" (Mount Vernon School 2018a). The next year, a student reached out to VR hardware creator Woojer to "clearly explain [their] goals and what [they] hoped for in a partnership with the company (Blumencranz 2019). Woojer eventually provided the VR Lab with one of their VR haptic vests. Sometimes reaching out to companies and making a compelling case for your partnership can lead to these kinds of resources for your VR space.

The end goal of cultivating an AR/VR/MR community through library programming and partnership is to form a sustainable AR/VR/MR group in which participants can share resources from all contributing partners and help each other instead of participants only expecting assistance from the service owners, teachers, or instructors. This community can build on the skills and availability of the many participants, rather than placing the weight on only one or two leaders.

APPLICABLE STANDARDS AS THEY RELATE TO COMMUNITY INTEGRATION

Effectively integrating community in your educational programming can benefit from following applicable educational standards from frameworks listed in Chapter 4. There are examples of standards with different focuses on different aspects of K–12 education.

Focusing on domains of competencies, the AASL Standards Framework for Learners lists standards of skill foundations and key commitment through the process of learning (American Association of School Librarians 2018).

- AASL. https://standards.aasl.org Find the complete standards at this link: https://standards.aasl.org/wp-content/uploads/2018/08/180206-AASL-framework-for-learners-2.pdf.

Focusing on content area studies, there is College, Career, and Civic Life (C3) Framework for social studies, CCSS Anchor Standards for Writing, and National Core Arts Standards (NCAS) for arts education (Swan et al 2013). C3 serves as a national guide for states to reference to upgrade their civic life education, and for school districts to strengthen their social studies programs (Houghton Mifflin Harcourt 2013). CCSS helps measure and prepare students' writing skills for college. And the NCAS provides guides of arts education from pre-K through high school with multiple examples of the standards put into practice for different grade levels Pre-K through High School (National Core Art Standards 2014).

- C3. https://c3teachers.org Find detailed information about the standards at this link https://www.socialstudies.org/system/files/2022/c3-framework-for-social-studies-rev0617.2.pdf.

- CCSS Anchor Standards for Writing for College and Career Readiness. Find the standards at http://www.corestandards.org.
- NCAS—Media Arts. The Media Arts standards can be found in PDF form at https://www.nationalartsstandards.org/sites/default/files/Media%20Arts%20at%20a%20Glance%20-%20new%20copyright%20info.pdf.

Focusing on technology, International Society for Technology in Education (ISTE) has a series of standards to help guide utilizing technologies in learning (ISTE 2016). Empowered Learner emphasizes students understanding technologies and using them for their personal learning goals. Digital Citizen raises students' awareness on positive, safe, legal and ethical digital behaviors and the potential impact of them on students' personal information.

- ISTE. Note that each standard contains four specific subskills that students might be using. Detailed descriptions of each student standard can be found at this link: https://www.iste.org/standards/iste-standards-for-students.

When creating an AR/VR/MR program, depending on the research focus and learning objectives, it is wise to select and combine components of different standards as applicable to guide the design of lesson plans and mentoring students through the learning experience.

CONCLUDING STATEMENTS ABOUT COMMUNITY

Creating new library programs and services have had two layers of challenges: lack of resources such as funds for equipment, and skilled support from specialized staff. Forming campus and external partnerships is an effective way of quickly gaining access to resources and support from other experts on campus. Equipment sharing programs offer great opportunities for libraries to leverage the use of other departments' devices. At the same time, libraries offer their partners the opportunity of exposing their resources to a wider user group beyond departmental boundaries, thus increasing community interest. Equally important, if not more, to a technology-heavy service such as AR/VR/MR program, is the expertise to drive the use of these devices. This is especially difficult at the adoption stage since not one single unit in an organization would have the skills to do it all. Therefore, sharing of expertise is imperative in the process of building up organizational capacity in using technical resources for teaching and research. By encouraging researchers, enthusiasts, and technologists to collaborate, we combine more interdisciplinary intelligence to facilitate collective learning. Community building activities within libraries have the potential to make a student's educational experience more impactful.

Libraries have unique advantages in building such programs and services. As a central space on campus supporting interdisciplinary research and services, the library has the ability to organically bring a diverse group of campus users together in one place outside of formal academic environments. Technologies like AR/VR/MR will promote themselves when people see them in action. Demonstrating these technologies in an open and interdisciplinary space like libraries with busy traffic gives them the optimal exposure to the whole community.

While consolidating resources and leveraging partnerships external to the organization, it is also advisable to set the boundaries at the beginning to avoid confusion and service expectation misalignment. Some considerations include agreement on: space usage requirements, equipment usage parameters, activities hosted, and what data is collected and shared. Agreement on space, time, activities, responsibilities, and information sharing assist with optimal resource allocation and helps the library stay focused on the activities within scope. Additionally, this establishes that all parties are willing to and capable of taking the responsibilities given and that the resulting workflow is smooth while providing the users with an enriching educational experience. Libraries also want to ensure that the data collected about these services abides by the organizational standards and is ethically and legally valid.

See the end of the chapter for a list of starter questions for your end-of-project report.

REFERENCES

American Association of School Librarians. 2018. "AASL standards framework for learners." *American Library Association*. https://standards.aasl.org/wp-content/uploads/2018/08/180206-AASL-framework-for-learners-2.pdf.

Blumencranz, Justin. 2019. "Justin Blumencranz helps take MV's virtual reality lab to the next level." *The Mount Vernon School*, May 1. https://mountvernonschool.org/justin-blumencranz-helps-take-mvs-virtual-reality-lab-to-the-next-level/.

Georgia Institute of Technology. n.d. "Center for 21st century universities." *Georgia Institute of Technology*. https://c21u.gatech.edu/.

Georgia State University. n.d. "Open world Atlanta." Georgia State University Student Innovation Fellowship Program. https://studentinnovation.gsucreate.org/projects/open-world-atlanta/.

Graham, Marie. 2019. "Hospital pain to beach carnival fun: Immersive technology to distract pediatric rehab patients." *The Mount Vernon School*, May 22. https://mountvernonschool.org/hospital-pain-to-beach-carnival-fun-immersive-technology-to-distract-pediatric-rehab-patients/.

Houghton Mifflin Harcourt. 2013. "Understanding the college, career, and civic life (C3) framework for social studies state standards." https://www.hmhco.com/~/media/sites/home/education/global/pdf/c3/c3_framework_white_paper.pdf?la=en.

Houston, Chip. 2019. "A celebration of upper school's mod 2." *The Mount Vernon School*, November 6. https://mountvernonschool.org/a-celebration-of-upper-schools-mod-2/.

ISTE. 2016. "ISTE standards: Students." https://www.iste.org/standards/iste-standards-for-students.

Kinberg, Margot. 2020. "Real-life nature-based experiences as keys to the writing workshop." *Networks: An Online Journal for Teacher Research* 22 (1). https://doi.org/10.4148/2470-6353.1308.

Mount Vernon School. 2017. "Partnering with Dell Alienware, MV students create virtual reality lab." *The Mount Vernon School*, November 1. https://mountvernonschool.org/partnering-with-dell-alienware-mv-students-create-virtual-reality-lab/.

Mount Vernon School. 2018a. "MV students & Dell Alienware officially launch virtual reality lab." *The Mount Vernon School*, April 11. https://mountvernonschool.org/mv-students-dell-alienware-officially-launch-virtual-reality-lab/.

Mount Vernon School. 2018b. "Students create virtual reality exhibit for the Center for Civil & Human Rights honoring Dr. King's legacy." *The Mount Vernon School*, August 22. https://mountvernonschool.org/students-create-virtual-reality-exhibit-for-the-center-for-civil-human-rights-honoring-dr-kings-legacy/.

Mount Vernon School. 2020. "Upper school virtual reality students partner with Children's Healthcare of Atlanta." *The Mount Vernon School*, January 15. https://mountvernonschool.org/upper-school-virtual-reality-students-partner-with-childrens-healthcare-of-atlanta/.

Mount Vernon School. 2022. "Lower school spring expeditions spark curiosities." *The Mount Vernon School*, May 18. https://mountvernonschool.org/ls-spring-expeditions/.

National Core Art Standards. 2014. "Media arts at a glance—New copyright info." Dover, DE: State Education Agency Directors of Art Education, National Coalition for Core Arts Standards. https://www.nationalartsstandards.org/sites/default/files/Media%20Arts%20at%20a%20Glance%20-%20new%20copyright%20info.pdf.

Neylon, Matthew. 2019. "Students create immersive art experience using virtual reality and music." *The Mount Vernon School*, September 11. https://mountvernonschool.org/students-create-immersive-art-experience-using-virtual-reality-and-music/.

PBLWorks. n.d. "What is PBL?" https://www.pblworks.org/what-is-pbl.

Penn Medicine. 2017. "Art courses could help medical students become better clinical observers." September 6. https://www.pennmedicine.org/news/news-releases/2017/september/art-courses-could-help-medical-students-become-better-clinical-observers.

Prohl, Benjamin M. 2022. "Project based learning as a tool for improved student engagement." Northwestern College, Iowa NWCommons Master's Theses & Capstone Projects Education. Spring 2022.

Strauss, Valerie. 2017. "The surprising thing Google learned about its employees—and what it means for today's students." *The Washington Post*, December 20. https://www.washingtonpost.com/news/answer-sheet/wp/2017/12/20/the-surprising-thing-google-learned-about-its-employees-and-what-it-means-for-todays-students/.

Swan, Kathy, and C3 Framework Writing Team. 2013. *The college, career, and civic life (C3) framework for social studies state standards: Guidance for enhancing the rigor of K-12 civics, economics, geography, and history.* Silver Spring, MD: National Council for the Social Studies. https://www.socialstudies.org/system/files/2022/c3-framework-for-social-studies-rev0617.2.pdf.

RESOURCES

Identifying Community Partners

What organizations and resources exist in your community that could be potential partners? Use this space to write down ideas and identify contact persons for those organizations.

____

____

____

____

____

____

____

Starter Questions to Ask Peer Institutions

- Did you start small and build up, or did you jump in the deep end?
- Do you offer augmented reality, virtual reality, or other technology?
- Have the types of immersive tech changed as the program has grown?
- How are AR/VR projects integrated into the existing curriculum?
- How much do your students know when they get started? How do you scaffold learning? How do you cater to different skill groups?
- What was one of the most interesting projects or outcomes from this initiative?
- Who do students turn to with technical questions?
- How do you manage software and hardware updates?
- What logistical strategies do you use for students checking out materials or using software and hardware outside of class time?
- Any other challenges and how did you address them?
- How do you share your creations with stakeholders, community partners, or other students?
- What was the greatest challenge in this initiative?
- Is there any particular software or hardware you would strongly recommend exploring at this time?

Project-Proposal Components for Student Projects

Students can use these points to develop their project proposal for an emerging technology-related student project.

- Abstract or overview of the project (business case)
- Team members and expected roles
- Resources and technology expected to be used
- Resources or technologies the library could support or help with, if applicable
- Proposed timeline with self-defined deadlines and brief description of activities
- Descriptive, including goals of the project and what you hope to accomplish, and how you might measure the success of your project
- Expected deliverables
- Expected challenges. What do you expect will be the biggest hurdles in your project? Risks involved?

End-of-Project-Report Components for Student Projects

Have students use interim reports and status reports to inform the final report. This makes the documentation process much more streamlined. Students can use these points to develop their end-of-project report or summary report for an emerging technology-related student project.

- Log major milestones in the project development
- Major challenges and how you addressed them
- The role team members played (if applicable)
- Technologies and software used and why
- Narrative or purpose of your project
- Any user feedback or user experience testing results you received
- Location of documents and/or files relevant to project
- How the final project differs from the proposal and why (if applicable)
- Next steps or possible improvements
- Any existing research referenced or sources used
- Links to any online resources used

SIX

Clearing the Hurdles: Initiating Programs That Utilize Emerging Technologies

The previous chapters laid out an outline for developing an emerging technology–focused program or service in a higher-education institution and in a K–12 school. This chapter will review some of the challenges more commonly encountered in the process and provide recommendations on how to overcome or avoid them.

STAKEHOLDER BUY-IN

In the process of developing a program, one of the early hurdles is developing stakeholder buy-in with administration, technology support, or other educator partnerships. Some strategies listed here can be effective selling points, depending on each colleague's research interests, specialties, and their willingness to take risks.

Some stakeholders might be very motivated by funding and budget information. As the program gets started, budget alternatives can be useful. Grants can be hit or miss, so pursuing multiple options, including small community offerings if that is appropriate for your organization, is a strategy to mitigate risk. It's important to be flexible about the scale of the initiatives you are trying to accomplish, considering that the full amount of funding may not be granted.

Other stakeholders might be interested in how the program will support their current work. For these individuals, pitching the program in a way that highlights personal research interests can be the connection point. Some programs are collaborative in nature, while others are very siloed and protective of their resources. Consider the context within your institution to make the best connections.

Another potential challenge that can occur when partnering with others is managing communal and individual resources. This is especially important if the program involves sharing spaces, hardware, software, or other technology elements. While it's difficult to plan every possible outcome or snag, it can be beneficial to review mutual expectations with different partners before beginning the project. For the space, review how and when your students will have access to the location, how the space should look when you leave, and what baseline behavioral rules exist for the space. Similarly for the hardware, review how and when your students will be able to access the resources. It is highly advisable to have a plan for what to do if items are broken or consequences if they are left in an unsuitable state. For software, review any available organizational guidelines for cybersecurity and digital citizenship. If there is a gap in these guidelines, there is an opportunity to consider instituting them for your program. (Find more information about digital citizenship in Chapter 3 and a later section of this chapter.)

It can be useful to review and clarify IT support commitment, if applicable. First, split the support of hardware and software responsibilities between the IT team and the service managers. For instance, the IT department might manage computers, user, and institutional accounts, but leave software testing or the piloting of specific VR headsets and computer peripheries to your program instructors. Second, the IT department might be able to help with an environmental scan to identify available resources within the library or in the organization, such as workstations, computer labs, 1:1 laptops, mobile devices, institutional accounts, and similar resources. Ongoing communication with IT partners can also cover how your institution acquires technology hardware or software and any existing procedures for assigning materials to students or lending materials to students. Third, the IT department, or other academic technology service personnel, might want to visit your class to review cybersecurity, ethics, and digital citizenship skills with your students. They might also provide institutionally accurate information for you to share with your students. The review can include procedures for passwords, downloads, updates, plug-ins, and error messages. This information can protect your class, students, and institution. Finally, it can be helpful to establish the boundaries of how the IT department can and cannot support your program. This might include available time windows, ticketing procedures, or device lending policies.

For institutions that do not have an in-house IT department, remote support options or crowdsourced resources are some of the alternative options to consider. Careful and succinct keyword searching can help you drill down and find the resources you need through a search engine. Question-and-answer message boards like Stack Overflow can help with coding challenges. The customer support teams for individual VR or AR devices might vary in their responsiveness but can provide customized support for their products.

STUDENT HESITANCY AND TECHNOLOGY PHOBIA

It's a misnomer that older adults are the only ones that suffer from technophobia or computer anxiety. The idea of the digital native is a myth. Marc Prensky first coined the term "digital native," referring to people born after 1980, with the implication that digital natives would be more adept at picking up new technology (2001). However, research indicates there is no significant difference between people born after 1980 and older generations regarding their skill or views about using technology (Kirschner and De Bruyckere 2017). In this chapter, as we discuss the most significant challenges or hurdles in integrating emerging technologies into your library's programming, we must address student reticence about working with new technologies. Students' worries can be lessened and confidence built by providing a scaffolded framework that supports their growing skill set. Keep in mind that the students' experiences and comfort levels in using technology will vary greatly. Factors such as peer influence, socioeconomic status, culture, and prior educational experiences can all impact a person's self-perceptions about their technical or creative abilities, more so than age.

Generally, people will only adopt and work with new technologies when they can see a clear benefit to using these new tools and resources (Toledo 2007). If students are unable to visualize the value-add from utilizing AR/VR/MR, it can lead to a lack of engagement or added anxiety about using the technology. One way to combat this initial ambiguity that can arise from not knowing what you don't know is, in a sense, to begin your project at the end. Visualizing real-world case studies and their advantages while discussing the positive by-products of working with emerging technologies can spawn discussions and, more importantly, prompt questioning from the students that will lay the foundation for their project plans or ideas. Allowing the students to see what is possible and using those case studies as inspiration will give them their initial building blocks for ideation. When reviewing project proposals, perhaps student ambitions are too high or the scope of the proposed project is not feasible for any number of reasons. Working with the students to create a scaled-down version of their ideas or designing exercises that provide students with quick wins can assist in increasing their comfort with technology. Therefore, an early consideration in dealing with technophobia is to assist your students in seeing a clear benefit to using the technology. Second, make a version of that benefit attainable within your time frame. For example, if a student wants to create a virtual tour of a lab space for remote users, perhaps adjust the scope to have the student create an interactive environment including only one piece of equipment initially. Having the student focus on a very simple manageable goal first will create natural positive reinforcement that demonstrates benefit and provides motivation for the next level of knowledge building.

Another strategy for overcoming the presence of technology anxiety is the integration of play. As mentioned earlier, play can bring together cognitive, emotional, and psychomotor elements of learning, making the learning experience a more holistic one. Play in general has been found to relieve tension and manage anxiety in K–12 students (Toledo 2007). Providing a low-stakes environment where the students can play games (both fun and educational) allows individuals of all ages to interact with the technologies in a setting where grades are not a major consideration. This could take the form of after-hours meetups, interest groups, clubs, and other extracurricular activities. Play provides a parallel channel that complements in-class activities and increases familiarity with technology. Integrating the element of fun alongside classes or programs, with no attachment to grades, is a light way to build initial engagement. In addition to playing games for fun, examples of play in education might be a virtual scavenger hunt in the style of Pokémon Go (Smith and Hottinger 2018) or working with artists to create retro-style posters with 3D anaglyph glasses or creating your own stereoscopic cards for use with a stereoscope (see Figures 6-1 and 6-2). The library is an ideal setting to bring play, tactile experiences, and academics together to enhance the learning experience.

Figure 6-1 Students created their own versions of the classic stereoscopic cards for use with vintage stereoscopes.

Figure 6-2 Students created themed anaglyph-style posters for use with 3D red and blue anaglyph paper glasses, making the images appear three-dimensional.

There is evidence to suggest that technology anxiety decreases with increased exposure or experience with such technologies (Ursavaş and Karal 2009). But how will novice users and students gain exposure to technologies outside of a classroom setting? This is a particularly important question to ask if they come from a socioeconomic background that doesn't readily allow them to sign up for extracurricular computing classes or to buy their own expensive equipment. Academic, school, and public libraries are expanding their services to include access to resources beyond books and journals. Service expansion includes access to advanced technologies. Libraries are evolving to meet the needs of current educational technologies. For instance, Georgia Tech offers a robust computer accessories and peripherals lending program; the library also offers a broad range of multimedia and data visualization software workshops (Georgia Tech, n.d.). The technologies are critical to communication skills and data analysis, and they are standard in nearly every industry. These services support the campus curriculum and prepare students for the competencies they may need in both classes and their careers. Therefore, libraries should continue to provide free or low-cost equal access to spaces, services, or labs that encourage children and adults alike to experiment and explore new technologies. By reducing obstacles and increasing the opportunity for users to gain experiences through experimentation, libraries can play a key role in decreasing the possibility that individuals will experience technophobia in classes or evaluative environments.

Student-centric learning transfers a certain level of control over the students' educational experience from the teacher to the student. Providing them with a flexible framework in which to learn contributes to reducing student anxiety surrounding new topics. When people are presented with a range of different ways to learn, they can choose methods that best help them to learn (Puteh and Ibrahim 2010). Student-centric learning fosters an environment that leads to more peer-to-peer knowledge exchange. "Peer-assisted learning (PAL) has been described as the development of knowledge and skill through active help and support among status equals or matched companions" (Glynn et al. 2006). Yildiz Durak's study in 2021 found the group that provided the most significant contribution to reducing technology anxiety was the peer-assisted learning group, when comparing peer-assisted, collaborative group learning and individual learning in a flipped classroom (Yildiz Durak 2022). Student-centric learning, as we've discussed in examples, is a model that allows students to take part in designing their own learning objectives and emphasizes process over end product. This framework can reduce anxiety surrounding the use of new technologies. In the resources at the end of the chapter, we share a few activities you can implement with students to assist in building confidence and reducing technology-related anxiety.

MAXIMIZING EXISTING RESOURCES AND TECHNOLOGY

An easy way to start a library initiative is to maximize the use of existing resources. Libraries, whether public, school, or academic, are to some extent underfunded. As a result of often limited funds, it can be hard to get leadership buy-in for experimenting with new ideas or adding new services. Utilizing existing resources is a great way of lowering your organization's financial burdens and increasing the chance of getting stakeholders' buy-in.

An environmental scan of your organization, your community, external partners, and professional groups could give you a list of resources available. At Georgia Tech, the librarians started experimenting with AR/VR in 2017 by merging the resources within an existing pilot Data Visualization lab. The sharing of resources spared the AR/VR program from committing to expense on new space or furniture. The librarians went further to use two existing workstations in the Data Visualization lab with upgraded graphic cards for development. Using the existing space and workstations lowered the cost to around $2,000 to test their new use cases.

The same philosophy was used when developing resources for the students to use in the research classes. After the class started, the librarians searched campus to locate appropriate hardware and expertise to enrich the learning experience. One good example, as mentioned earlier, was one of the early projects that required the students to create 3D models to incorporate into a virtual environment. The librarians were able to locate a high-resolution 3D scanner on campus through another department for the scanning task. This department offered assistance and equipment. Through this process, these educational partners learned about additional use cases for their equipment, making the experience mutually beneficial. For libraries that want to do the same, reaching out to other branches of your organization or a local makerspace may bring back surprising and useful resources. Again, this emphasizes the importance of strategic partnerships that benefit student learning.

For beginners of AR/VR/MR development, it eases the learning curve and workload by using as many existing models as possible. One popular resource is the Unity Asset Store. It offers a robust collection of 2D and 3D models, templates, and other development tools—a large number of which are free or offered at a very low cost. Your local libraries and archives would have a rich collection of local culture and history, if that relates to your project design. In the Georgia Tech VR campus tour project mentioned earlier, students used scans of images and artifacts from the institute archives. There are also online archives and creative commons licenses that can provide images and scans to add to your projects. Music is another important component. There are online services that provide free music and sound effects. Free Music Archive (https://freemusicarchive.org/) and New Media Rights (https://www.newmediarights.org/) are two popular ones.

Students can go even further to use some existing apps to create their models. One good example with HTC VIVE is the app *Tilt Brush*. This app can be used to create artistic content that can be downloaded and used in student projects. To further enrich your project options, finding local resources for project content is also worth exploring. At Georgia Tech, we returned to the archives semester after semester for artifacts, newspapers, old images, and more to be added to our projects. This not only brings in rich cultural components to our projects, it also enables better access to and deep exploration of archival materials for the viewers (Pellerin, Mi, and Valk 2019).

There are also online platforms students can browse for project inspiration. The biggest platforms of this sort include Google Earth VR, YouTube VR, and Within (www.with.in). These platforms collectively offer a variety of projects developed with different hardware, using different content, and at different technical levels. By browsing these websites students can gain insights of project possibilities and hopefully connect that to their own designs.

In addition to tools and assets readily available, there could also be human capital in your organization, or in professional or online communities, that you can collaborate with and learn from. Returning to our 3D model creation experience, if you need to create 3D models with scanners external to your organization, check to see if there is a staff member or specialist willing to help you get started using the scanner and editing software. 3D modeling and scanning especially requires patience through trial and error. Guidance at the beginning of the process while familiarizing your team with specialized tools could save people hours, if not more. There is also a wealth of AR/VR development on various online forums. Some of the most active ones include Unity Forums (https://forum.unity.com/), Oculus

Community (https://forums.oculusvr.com/t5/Oculus-Community/ct-p/oculus-community), and StackOverflow (https://stackoverflow.com/). With broad technical user groups, frequently these forums have already seen technical questions you will encounter. Other users may have responded with a ready list of solutions. If your question is new, you have the opportunity of having other fellow developers look at it and give your suggestions.

DOCUMENTATION STRATEGIES

Documentation is important for program or service managers, instructors, and students alike, not only to record processes and technical steps in the moment, but also as a tool for preserving collective knowledge over time. Effective documentation strategies allow service managers to easily hand off work instructions to others in their absence, and it assists others in understanding the basis for the current level of service. These same strategies give instructors the ability to preserve their course design and remix teaching strategies from semester to semester, thus keeping content customized and up-to-date to reflect current learning objectives. For students, effective documentation helps them build on the knowledge of prior students, as well as showcasing their research.

As we consider the importance of knowledge management, the next hurdle to anticipate is how best to document and preserve both instructors' and students' work. Although every situation is different, there are a few key concepts that can apply across settings. Libraries are an ideal setting to impart to students the unique challenges of preserving and organizing digital content over time. In our institution's research classes and programming there is a heavy emphasis on documenting, reflection, maintaining adequate backups, and consistent naming conventions.

For instructors, developing a class framework that can be used and reused to accommodate students' new concepts and proposals each semester will both be efficient for the instructor and promote student-centric learning. If students are proposing an idea or a course project, consider structuring the documentation strategy with elements of project management to:

- Submit a business case
- Submit use cases that outline the benefits and ethical considerations
- Define scope
- Outline resources

- List possible challenges or risks
- Establish tentative timeline and milestones
- Report ongoing status updates

Project status updates are an effective way of tracking the project progress. As the students progress in their research, project status updates reflect the difference between the proposal and the reality of their work. If major changes are needed for the project scope or the deliverables, instructors can incorporate milestones mid-semester that provide students with an opportunity to submit a change request and modify the expected final deliverables. Although these project management skills may seem tedious to the students, they will appreciate clear expectations such as the time commitment of each step, deliverables, and alternative solutions if necessary. In addition to project outlines, students working on group projects that involve AR/VR/MR should always document clear assignment of team member roles on each task. Transparency equals accountability, and having the students sign a contract that they share with their group and instructors will encourage self-regulated behaviors and responsibility. This contract or agreement should be part of the documentation standards. These proposals should be reviewed, tracked, and stored. Project documentation can be saved on various cloud tools or a learning management system (e.g., Canvas) if your organization utilizes one.

A knowledge base of important skills and resources learned from the project is of great value to the class and future classes. As the project moves forward and workflow procedures are being tested, adopted, or abandoned, a knowledge base can facilitate collective access, editing, and preservation of this knowledge. Effective documentation should take software information into account and have consistent annotation. Software versions should be recorded for future reference as they update frequently. There should also be clear and consistent commenting to go with the code for readers. Since process is emphasized over end product, it will be important to emphasize that students document not only successes but the trial-and-error experience, as well. If a path was taken that ultimately did not work, that should be recorded to help future students to understand the execution process.

Finally, students are encouraged to reflect on the ethics in decision-making through the documentation. Corple et al. suggest "educators use reflexive principlism as a framework in this process, giving students language to use as they reflect. Doing so would help students make their intuitive decisions more explicit and enable them to reflect on their ethical decision-making" (2020). Based on this recommendation, giving students an index of terminology to use or a structure for decision-making would assist them in describing their work more comprehensively and further getting at the why, in addition to the how and the what of the project.

There are a variety of tools that can host the knowledge base. Wikis can be a simple and clean tool to share documentation over time. It allows the instructor to have admin rights to the documentation and easy transfer of the documentation from departing team members to new ones. MediaWiki (https://www.mediawiki.org/wiki/MediaWiki) is open source, free, and can be customized via plug-ins. DokuWiki (https://www.dokuwiki.org/dokuwiki) is a good option for users with low system requirements. It also has numerous plug-ins for the service as desired. One example is the GoogleDrawing plug-in. This plug-in lets users paste Google drawing links, and they will be shown as an image in the wiki. These types of plug-ins allow for flexibility in how the content is displayed. If students are creating initial ideation drawings, these too can be preserved. Plug-ins are to open-source software as apps are to your smartphone: they extend the basic functionality and allow the user to customize their experience. Researching and exploring extensions including templates and plug-ins can be part of the students' documentation workflow as they build out the platform. Other platforms that can be considered as a knowledge base host are open-source content management systems such as WordPress or Drupal to create a project or class website. Like wikis, these have extensions that allow users to customize the instance for their specific use cases. Unlike wikis, which may serve primarily as internal documentation, a website can be used to showcase student work and share final products publicly in a more polished format. Libraries can select some work to be preserved in the institute's digital repository. To echo the concept of community in Chapter 5, it is also helpful to have students share their work through a variety of channels.

Libraries also have resources to help disseminate AR/VR/MR research. Libraries have social media and videoblog presence; some even host or connect to academic podcasts. These are great sources for students to easily publish and distribute their research through different modalities. Some students may wish to document their "behind-the-scenes" work to later share with the AR/VR community. This encourages metacognition and a sense of pride in their project by attaching a documentary-style narrative to the student research. Mobilizing the rich resources in and around libraries to facilitate project preservation, sharing, and showcasing is a unique advantage the library should take to preserve and promote AR/VR/MR work and research in general.

IMPLEMENTING CHANGES BASED ON STUDENT INPUT

Student reflections at the end of the project are an excellent resource for identifying workflow challenges and indicating whether learning objectives were met. Reviewing this information with the project teams can benefit present and future students as well as improving the pedagogy surrounding the work. Conversations between instructors and students regarding the course design and learning outcomes can facilitate the cocreation of project rubrics, which gives students more agency over their learning journey. When students have a clear understanding of how they are being evaluated and what the learning objectives are, the greater the chances for success. In this way, when students have a greater say in designing their research projects and outlining project deliverables, the associated assessment methods factor the students as individuals and the originality of their proposals. Therefore, there are no right or wrong answers; it is simply a learning experience.

As we referenced earlier, one of the roles we envision for the instructor is to provide the students with the structure or the language to effectively reflect on their learning experiences. Therefore, having the instructor provide prompts can make these reflections more impactful. One such approach and framework may be to align reflective activities with Bloom's taxonomy (Whalen and Paez 2019).

Having reflective activities count as a part of the grade and increasing the students' awareness of the language can improve communication skills and allow them to self-examine their work more thoroughly. For this reason, it is beneficial to have an activity built into the course where students practice drafting statements that include terminology appropriate to Bloom's. Additionally, have them categorize their statements to improve metacognition.

1. *Remember:* I was able to *recall* the location to find 3D assets for my project.
2. *Understand:* Having read the assigned article, our team was able to *compare* the features of different types of headsets.
3. *Apply:* Our team was able to *construct* a section of the project website that explains our project goals. We also organized workflow instructions for the wiki and *modified* project code after debugging.

4. *Analyze:* I *evaluated* our onboarding process and integrated it into our workflow. Along with teammates, we streamlined that process for new students on the team.
5. *Evaluate:* After comparing Unity's collaboration tools and preserving our work via GitHub, we *assessed* that GitHub would be easier to maintain due to ongoing updates from Unity.
6. *Create:* We *designed* a game that allows the user to experience aspects of our culture. We also *created* a manual and accompanying documentation that follows our work and explains how to begin the game.

Whalen et al. state that "working within a pre-defined hierarchy and widely accepted framework offered a legitimate way to effectively assess and evaluate learning as well as to more effectively communicate the desired outcomes to the students" (2019). They go on to say, "Bloom's taxonomy also addresses the need for institutions to measure and report program-level learning outcomes by enabling instructors to measure and report on course-level learning outcomes" (Whalen and Paez 2019).

If students have revelations that improve workflow, or point out key tasks that optimize the development process, or make statements that crystalize understanding, these are valuable contribution toward redesigning and adapting the next version of a project or class.

Student reflection can be presented in a variety of modes and formats. Digital storytelling has been used as an educational tool to form learning communities, in a variety of educational settings, but it can also be used as a mode for student reflection. Austen, Pickering, and Judge discuss that "digital storytelling has also been used to aid reflection both in learning and socially through peer critique. The process of storytelling and digital production can allow students to connect to the affective component of their learning" (2021). Additionally, "digital storytelling has been found to be effective as an inclusive assessment" (Austen, Pickering, and Judge 2021). Digital storytelling allows students an opportunity to analyze and share personal observations in a way that might not otherwise be possible through a traditional written report or essay. Finally, one important aim of digital storytelling is to amplify hidden or marginalized voices. Digital storytelling can provide students with a unique way to reflect on their research process and learning journey. Students could create anything from a short documentary style video outlining their work to a podcast or animated slide show that explains success and failures along the way. Depending on the type of media the student was creating, software that could be used for these reflective activities could include Audacity, PowToons, Adobe Express, iMovie, and PowerPoint, to name a few. Digital storytelling can be an inclusive tool for gathering feedback as well as one that promotes reflective thinking and metacognition during the research process.

Student reflections are a resource for both student and teacher. By integrating this feedback into your course design and continually improving on the pedagogy, you will set the team up for success. Reflections can take the form of a final report or many other formats to promote inclusive assessment.

PROJECT COLLABORATION AND PRESERVATION

As with any other format of digital scholarship, research generated with technologies of the XR family need supporting tools throughout the research data life cycle, namely, collaboration tools during the project and preservation options after completion.

As far as collaboration is concerned, the standard platform for coding is GitHub, which is an online service to save, edit, share, publish, and update code among team members. At Georgia Tech, the library instructors have recommended it to students in the past, but none of the projects used it extensively. Students complained that it was not intuitive to use for their projects without clear articulation. Later we came to realize that most of the students were in their sophomore or junior years, with limited internship and real-world project experience. Thus, their knowledge of GitHub was nonexistent, despite being at an engineering school. It does take some effort to start using GitHub: process-wise, it requires downloading and installing GitHub Desktop; skill-wise, students need to learn a list of commands to execute tasks. For a hands-on learning experience like our class, it is important to not only walk learners through the essential tools they need to create their project, like Unity and Blender; it is equally important to get them started with supporting tools like GitHub. Further training on the tool, therefore, has the potential of fueling online collaboration, allowing more flexible work schedules, and enabling accurate tracking and version control of the projects.

After the projects are completed, there need to be preservation options to save the projects for future showcasing and learning. Digital preservation, according to the Association for Library Collections and Technical Services Preservation and Reformatting Section of the American Library

Association, is combining "policies, strategies and actions that ensure access to digital content over time" (ALCTS 2008). The need for digital preservation arises due to the short life span of hard drives, which is especially true for emerging technologies such as AR and VR. Intellectually, preserving AR/VR research is new territory that is not yet widely explored in academia. Some questions that need to be discussed include:

- How to select projects for preservation?
- What is the policy for short/medium/long-term preservation?
- What are the technical platforms for such efforts?

Practically, there are limited preservation options for AR/VR projects, most of which are for large-scale significant research (Tate, n.d.).

A main challenge of preserving and rendering projects built on AR/VR devices is that "due to the rapidly evolving commercial landscape of VR manufacturing, hardware components are at high risk of obsolescence, threatening the sustainability of VR systems" (Ensom and McConchie 2021), and by that very fact, the sustainability of projects built on them. For libraries and other educational organizations that want to save the students' work for later display, the tools are sparce. There are two main categories of preservation tools available now. One category of tools targets large-scale projects with cultural and scholarly significance (Ansom and McConchie 2021). These platforms, if not customized for just one project, are focused on a specific area, such as cultural heritage or artworks. Other options for preserving AR/VR projects are proprietary hosts, such as the Oculus Store or the Android App Store. These stores also have their limitations in terms of required project quality and cost commitment. Due to the nature of students' work, none of these categories would match the need of an open platform easily saving, retrieving, maintaining and rendering the content at low or no cost. As a result, this should be taken into consideration, and we recommend exploring the availability of appropriate options for preservation during the design and planning phase of any new service or before beginning research work.

SECURITY, SAFETY, AND ACCESS

As elaborated in Chapter 3, cybersecurity and education on the subject are becoming an important part of any technology-driven learning experience, and therefore, a major challenge and opportunity for AR/VR/MR education. The Cybersecurity and Infrastructure Security Agency (CISA) has a K–12 School Security Guide and Web-based School Security Assessment Tool that "provide schools with a comprehensive doctrine and methodology to assess vulnerabilities, plan for emergencies, and implement layered elements of security" (CISA 2022). Public schools and libraries in the United States likely fall under the Children's Internet Protections Act, which requires that "they are enforcing a policy of Internet safety that includes measures to block or filter Internet access for both minors and adults to certain visual depictions" and that the organization's "policy of Internet safety includes monitoring the online activities of minors" in general (GA DOE, n.d.). Sections that are relevant to VR projects include addressing "access by minors to inappropriate matter on the Internet," "the safety and security of minors when using . . . chat rooms and other forms of direct electronic communications," "unlawful activities by minors online" (hacking), "unauthorized . . . dissemination of personal information regarding minors," and "measures designed to restrict minors' access to materials harmful to minors" (GA DOE, n.d.). Six federal departments and agencies, including the U.S. Department of Education, collaborated to create the "Guide for Developing High-Quality School Emergency Operations Plans," which recommends an ongoing "six-step planning process" for multiple kinds of school threats, including cyber ones. The plan distinguishes between "cybersecurity (i.e., IT systems and networks) and cyber safety (i.e., the human element)" (REMS TA Center 2017, 5).

The first step toward safe cyber behavior is to educate the educators about cyber risks. A few of the threats relating to VR technologies include (1) unpatched or outdated software that can allow unauthorized access to information networks (REMS TA Center 2017, 3), (2) illegitimate software downloads, or (3) illegitimate software that is disguised as legitimate software in order to distribute malware. Removable storage devices can be stolen or corrupted and thus infect information networks with malware (REMS TA Center 2017, 2). Additionally, if student users are connected to the Internet, malicious users may use social engineering methods to extract personally identifiable information from them. The major approaches to raising general cybersecurity awareness, as stated in Quayyum, Cruzes, and Jaccheri's study (2021, 13), are:

- Training (informative video, interactive presentation, digital comics, school curriculum, privacy management tools, password strategies)
- Game-based learning (privacy-related games and stories, AR-based serious game, mobile game)

- Intervention (workshop or educational camp)
- Gamification
- Warning
- Negotiation of cybersecurity within family home
- One-stop solution mobile app

The next step is to incorporate cybersecurity into classroom practice to help raise students' awareness. The National Institute of Standards and Technology (NIST) has a list of recommendations for "protecting controlled unclassified information in nonfederal systems and organizations" that are relevant to developing a VR Lab. They include:

- Employ the principle of least privilege, where authorized privileges are "no higher than necessary to accomplish required organizational missions or business functions" (Ross et al. 2020, 12).
- Ensure that . . . users of organizational systems are made aware of the security risks associated with their activities and of the applicable policies, standards, and procedures related to the security of those systems (Ross et al. 2020, 16).
- Provide security awareness training on recognizing and reporting potential indicators of insider threat (Ross et al. 2020, 17).
- Restrict, disable, or prevent the use of nonessential programs, functions, ports, protocols, and services (Ross et al. 2020, 22).
- Control and monitor user-installed software (Ross et al. 2020, 23).
- Control the use of removable media on system components (Ross et al. 2020, 30).
- Periodically assess the security controls in organizational systems to determine if the controls are effective in their application (Ross et al. 2020, 34).

In an ideal setting, cybersecurity education can permeate multiple subjects in a student's day, not only during IT training or computing classes. For instance, there should be time for AR/VR/MR research classes dedicated to reviewing cybersecurity and digital citizenship considerations with students. Even if they have some education in this area, the review will recontextualize and refresh the information for the student users. Cyber behaviors and risks could also become part of a language arts or debate topic or be integrated into history discussions or science classes that use various technologies (Rahman et al. 2020, 380). Students can be active participants in their cyber well-being, protecting themselves from exterior threats, engaging in positive behavior themselves, and learning how to regulate their own use and engagement with technologies.

PROJECT MANAGEMENT

In this chapter, we have discussed various challenges and strategies associated with building a library program or service that incorporates immersive technologies such as AR/VR/XR. With all the expected and unexpected hurdles, it is critical to have a process in place to manage the workflow and delivery of service in a timely manner. This is where project management comes into play. According to Elam (2022) from Learning Tree, a project management training organization, a project is "a temporary endeavor undertaken to create a unique product, service or result to meet specific goals or objectives." In the context of building a library service, the project phase is when the service owners collect information, propose an initiative, get leadership approval, and put resources together to pilot the service until it's a maturely established operation. Project management is "the art and science of applying project management standards, best practices, techniques, templates, and tools to project work." After a concept is approved and the project is initiated, the project manager needs to form the project team of key stakeholders and collaborators, document the progress, delegate tasks to team members, and communicate the progress to all stakeholders.

Adopting project management in library management has multiple benefits. First, it creates a channel to bring innovative service or program ideas to the attention of library leadership. It is not uncommon that, without a process like project management in place, the leadership could potentially become disconnected from the daily library operation and arising service needs. This disconnection is likely worse for bigger libraries. Giving people the opportunities to propose project ideas and defend them in front of colleagues is a great way to converse about new service needs. Second, it brings all stakeholders, including leadership, service owners, facility teams, and IT teams, together for the design and implementation of a service effort. Going through the project management process requires all key stakeholders and collaborators to meet regularly, discuss the project details, and update each other about the process and changes, if any. Third, it has clearly defined a timeline for progress and completion, and resource commitment. From the whole project to different phases, such as initiation, implementation, testing, and handover, to specific tasks, such as drafting a service management plan and discussing furniture and space design, all have a defined timeline and resource allocation and are assigned to specific team members. Fourth, it creates regular and formal communication in person or online to make sure all team members are on the same page. Regular communication and thorough documentation about the project scope, time, and limitations helps manage stakeholders' expectations. Besides the project flow, the techniques of project management could also be used in the process of learning, as discussed in earlier sections.

Working with emerging technologies incorporates numerous factors and considerations. Ultimately, as libraries further incorporate AR/VR/MR into their programming, we strive to have these technologies expand and improve how libraries can serve their respective communities. The goal being to enhance learning and positively impact the student experience while developing innovative research concepts. Our examples in some cases are unique to an organization's local ecosystem. However, this book can be used as a blueprint to develop your own specialized programs while taking into account the requirements of one's own institution. Please reference the resources at the end of each chapter as you go through the steps of service development. Each resource section offers a mixture of worksheets, questionnaires, diagrams, or checklists that correspond to the content covered in Chapters 2–6. Good luck making your virtual (augmented or mixed) reality dreams into reality!

REFERENCES

ALCTS. 2008. "Definitions of digital preservation." *American Library Association*, February 21. http://www.ala.org/alcts/resources/preserv/defdigpres0408.

Austen, L., N. Pickering, and M. Judge. (2021). "Student reflections on the pedagogy of transitions into higher education, through digital storytelling." *Journal of Further and Higher Education* 45 (3): 337–348.

CISA. 2022. "CISA releases updated K-12 school security guide and assessment tool." February 23. https://www.cisa.gov/news/2022/02/23/cisa-releases-updated-k-12-school-security-guide-and-assessment-tool.

Corple, D. J., Carla B. Zoltowski, Megan Kenny Feister, and Patrice M. Buzzanell. 2020. "Understanding ethical decision-making in design." *Journal of Engineering Education* 109: 262–280. https://doi.org/10.1002/jee.20312.

Elam, Christopher. 2022. "Course 4621: Project management fundamentals." Lecture, Georgia Institute of Technology Library, Atlanta, GA, August 2.

Ensom, Tom, and Jack McConchie. 2021. "Preserving Virtual Reality Artworks." Tate Modern, August 13. https://www.tate.org.uk/documents/54/tate_pim_preservingvrartworks_01_00.pdf

GA DOE. n.d. "Children's Internet Protections Act summary." https://www.gadoe.org/Technology-Services/Instructional-Technology/Pages/CIPA-Summary.aspx.

Georgia Tech. n.d. "Library." Georgia Institute of Technology. https://library.gatech.edu/.

Glynn, L. G., A. MacFarlane, M. Kelly, P. Cantillon, and A. W. Murphy. 2006. "Helping each other to learn—a process evaluation of peer assisted learning." *BMC Medical Education* 6: 18. https://doi.org/10.1186/1472-6920-6-18.

Kirschner, P., and P. De Bruyckere. 2017. "Digital natives are a myth." *Teaching and Teacher Education* 67: 135–142. https://www.rmit.edu.au/news/c4de/digital-natives-are-a-myth.

Pellerin, A., X. Mi, and A. Valk. 2019. "Realizing the past: Charting a course for sustainable instruction and engagement with archival materials using augmented and virtual reality technologies." *The Journal of Interactive Technology and Pedagogy* 14. https://jitp.commons.gc.cuny.edu/realizing-the-past-charting-a-course-for-sustainable-instruction-and-engagement-with-archival-materials-using-augmented-and-virtual-reality-technologies/

Prensky, Marc. 2001. "Digital natives, digital immigrants, part 1." *On the Horizon* 9: 3–6. http://dx.doi.org/10.1108/10748120110424816.

Puteh, Marzita, and Mahani Ibrahim. 2010. "The usage of self-regulated learning strategies among form four students in the mathematical problem-solving context: A case study." *Procedia Social and Behavioral Sciences* 8: 446–452. doi: 10.1016/j.sbspro.2010.12.061.

Quayyum, Farzana, Daniela S. Cruzes, and Letizia Jaccheri. 2021. "Cybersecurity awareness for children: A systematic literature review." *International Journal of Child-Computer Interaction* 30. https://doi.org/10.1016/j.ijcci.2021.100343.

Rahman, N. A. A, I. H. Sairi, N. A. M. Zizi, and F. Khalid. 2020. "The importance of cybersecurity education in school." *International Journal of Information and Education Technology* 10 (5): 378–382. doi: 10.18178/ijiet.2020.10.5.1393.

REMS TA Center. 2017. "Cybersecurity considerations for K-12 schools and school districts." Readiness and Emergency Management for Schools Technical Assistance Center. https://rems.ed.gov/docs/Cybersecurity_K-12_Fact_Sheet_508C.PDF.

Ross, Ron, Victoria Pillitteri, Kelley Dempsey, Mark Riddle, and Gary Guissanie. 2020. "Protecting controlled unclassified information in nonfederal systems and organizations." National Institute of Standards and Technology, Revision 2, February 2020. https://doi.org/10.6028/NIST.SP.800-171r2.

Smith, Kai Alexis, and Paul R. Hottinger. 2018. *Gotta catch 'em all. A case study about Cal Poly Pomona's Pokemon GO AR orientation.* Pomona: California State Polytechnic University. http://hdl.handle.net/10211.3/205336.

Tate. n.d. "Project: Preserving immersive media." September 2018—ongoing. https://www.tate.org.uk/about-us/projects/preserving-immersive-media.

Toledo, C. 2007. "Digital culture: Immigrants and tourists responding to the natives." *Drumbeat International Journal of Teaching and Learning in Higher Education* 19 (1): 84–92. https://www.isetl.org/ijtlhe/pdf/IJTLHE152.pdf.

Ursavaş, Ö. F., and H. Karal. 2009. "Assessing pre-service teachers' computer phobia levels in terms of gender and experience—Turkish." *International Journal of Behavioral, Cognitive, Educational and Psychological Sciences* 1 (1): 71–75.

Whalen, Kate, and Antonio Paez. 2019. "Development of a new framework to guide, assess, and evaluate student reflections in a university sustainability course." *Teaching and Learning Inquiry* 7 (1): 55–77. https://doi.org/10.20343/teachlearninqu.7.1.5.

Yildiz Durak, Hatice. 2022. "Flipped classroom model applications in computing courses: Peer-assisted groups, collaborative group and individual learning." *Computer Applications in Engineering Education* 30: 803–820. https://doi.org/10.1002/cae.22487.

RESOURCES

Building Confidence and Reducing Technology Anxiety

Media-related activities for beginners.

- *Students create a simple video,* introducing themselves to the class and uploading it to a video-sharing platform or learning management system with their smartphone; or if they don't have access to a smartphone, students can utilize device lending programs at public or academic libraries to get a basic recording device.
  - Take this a step further and have students integrate one overlay into their video with a simple editing platform such as iMovie. An example of an overlay is putting a string of text over a video frame. (Layering video)
- *A variation on the video activity could be having students create an audio narrative or short podcast.* Free tools such as Audacity can be used to integrate sound effects or layer music into a track.
- *Utilize drawing tablets.* Allowing students to create expressive drawings with a tablet, iPad, and software such as Adobe Fresco.
- *Select activities in Adobe Photoshop or Creative editing platforms.* Photo-editing tools can be complex; however, if you begin with some instant gratification exercises, you can instill confidence. Begin with activities that involve a minimum number of steps to achieve the desired result. For instance, *use of the magic eraser tool* to remove an unwanted object from the background of photograph.
- *Create a simple 3D object with Blocks and Google cardboard* (https://arvr.google.com/blocks/)
- *Use Google Cardboard* in conjunction with your smart device and 360 pictures.
- *Create a simple 1-minute stop-motion video* with an app such as iStopMotion.

Forums and Troubleshooting

- Other people in your organization
- Unity Forums, https://forum.unity.com/

- Oculus Community, https://forums.oculusvr.com/t5/Oculus-Community/ct-p/oculus-community
- Stack Overflow, https://stackoverflow.com/

Backups and Backward-Compatibility Checklist

- What is your collaboration tool to share and access code?
- Where are you going to preserve your project after completion?
- Do you plan to grant access to other people to play the game; if so, is there clear documentation of the tools used and version information?

Bloom's Taxonomy of Measurable Verbs

By creating learning objectives using measurable verbs, you indicate what the student must do to demonstrate learning. Further information can be found : Armstrong, P. (2010). Bloom's Taxonomy. Vanderbilt University Center for Teaching. https://cft.vanderbilt.edu/guides-sub-pages/blooms-taxonomy/.

Index

Page numbers followed by *t* indicate tables and *f* indicate figures.

About the Authors

ALISON VALK is the instructional coordinator and multimedia librarian for the Georgia Tech Library. She teaches approximately 100 workshops a year on professional multimedia software, including tools for AR/VR, video/audio editing, and graphic design. In 2016, she became the program manager for the Georgia Tech Library's instruction program and service owner of the library's Media Scholarship Commons. As instructional coordinator, she oversees the development of the library's educational curriculum. She leads numerous specialized educational programs that incorporate emerging technologies, as well as a federal Institute for Museum and Library Services grant-funded program that integrates arts-based projects and library resources into the curriculum.

XIMIN MI has been working on developing virtual reality library services since 2016. Since becoming the data visualization librarian at Georgia Tech Library in 2017, Mi has led the acquisition of VR devices and service development and co-taught the virtual reality undergraduate research section with colleague Alison Valk. She also focuses on developing library data services, teaches other classes and noncredit workshops, and provides research data consultation to campus students, faculty, and staff.

ASHLEY L. SCHICK is an artist and art educator. She taught drawing, printmaking, and digital photography in the upper school at the Lovett School, Atlanta, Georgia, where she also led cross-curricular projects, joining arts and technology with other disciplines. She was an active member of the Lovett Digital Citizenship Committee. Schick has taught workshops with SCAD, Georgia Tech, the Atlanta Printmakers Studio, the High Museum, the Atlanta Zine Fest, and other organizations. Her artwork has been exhibited nationally and internationally, has been installed in film sets, and is held in multiple private and university collections.